Engineering and Construction Contract

This contract should be used for the appointment of a contractor for engineering and construction work, including any level of design responsibility

An NEC document
June 2017
(with amendments October 2020)

The Government Construction Board, Cabinet Office UK

The Government Construction Board (formerly Construction Clients' Board) recommends that public sector organisations use the NEC contracts and in particular the NEC4 contracts where appropriate, when procuring construction. Standardising use of this comprehensive suite of contracts should help to deliver efficiencies across the public sector and promote behaviours in line with the principles of the Government Construction Strategy.

The Development Bureau, HKSAR Government

The Development Bureau recommends the progressive transition from NEC3 to NEC4 in public works projects in Hong Kong. With suitable amendments to adapt to the Hong Kong local environment, NEC4 is expected to further enhance collaborative partnering, unlock innovations and achieve better cost management and value for money in public works projects.

NEC is a division of Thomas Telford Ltd, which is a wholly owned subsidiary of the Institution of Civil Engineers (ICE), the owner and developer of the NEC.

The NEC is a suite of standard contracts, each of which has these characteristics:

* Its use stimulates good management of the relationship between the two parties to the contract and, hence, of the work included in the contract.

* It can be used in a wide variety of commercial situations, for a wide variety of types of work and in any location.

* It is a clear and simple document – using language and a structure which are straightforward and easily understood.

NEC4 Engineering and Construction Contract is one of the NEC suite and is consistent with all other NEC4 documents. Also available are the Engineering and Construction Contract User Guides, Flow Charts and Options A, B, C, D, E and F.

ISBN (complete box set) 978-0-7277-6391-4
ISBN (this document) 978-0-7277-6209-2
ISBN (Establishing a Procurement and Contract Strategy) 978-0-7277-6223-8
ISBN (Preparing an Engineering and Construction Contract) 978-0-7277-6224-5
ISBN (Selecting a Supplier) 978-0-7277-6234-4
ISBN (Managing an Engineering and Construction Contract) 978-0-7277-6235-1
ISBN (Engineering and Construction Contract Flow Charts) 978-0-7277-6267-2
ISBN (Option A: Priced contract with activity schedule) 978-0-7277-6311-2
ISBN (Option B: Priced contract with bill of quantities) 978-0-7277-6312-9
ISBN (Option C: Target contract with activity schedule) 978-0-7277-6313-6
ISBN (Option D: Target contract with bill of quantities) 978-0-7277-6314-3
ISBN (Option E: Cost reimbursable contract) 978-0-7277-6315-0
ISBN (Option F: Management contract) 978-0-7277-6316-7

Consultative edition 1991
First edition 1993
Second edition 1995
Third edition 2005, Reprinted with amendments 2013
Fourth edition June 2017
Reprinted with amendments January 2019
Reprinted with amendments October 2020
Reprinted 2021

British Library Cataloguing in Publication Data for this publication is available from the British Library.

Typeset by Manila Typesetting Company

Printed and bound in Great Britain by Bell & Bain Limited, Glasgow, UK

Contents

Foreword

Continuous improvement in project delivery is required to build confidence in the UK construction sector so that we can attract more investment. The Infrastructure and Projects Authority (IPA) is the government's centre of expertise for infrastructure and major projects. We sit at the heart of government, reporting to the Cabinet Office and HM Treasury.

The application of the right contract is central to the success of the overall project delivery system. The NEC suite of contracts has been in existence for over the 20 years and has linked the projects, people and processes together to create the correct environment for successful delivery.

This new and updated NEC4 contract embraces the digital changes that are happening in the construction industry, especially around BIM, which I believe will be central to creating a step change in performance. Whilst looking forward it also builds on the fundamentals required for an effective contract.

The use of NEC4 on public sector projects will help to deliver the Government Construction Strategy as we seek to improve central government's capability as a construction client to deliver further savings in the order of £1.7bn across the Government estate. The IPA looks forward to collaborating with industry to make the delivery of projects more efficient and effective.

Tony Meggs, Chief Executive, Infrastructure and Projects Authority

Infrastructure
and Projects
Authority

Reporting to Cabinet Office
and HM Treasury

Preface

NEC was first published as a new and innovative way of managing construction contracts in 1993 – some 24 years ago. It was designed to facilitate and encourage good management of risks and uncertainties, using clear and simple language.

The NEC approach to managing contracts was endorsed in "Constructing the team – The Latham Report", which was a government/industry review of procurement and contractual arrangements in the UK construction industry. This led to a second edition in 1995 incorporating the further recommendations of that review. This contract was used increasingly in the UK and overseas, and a major revision was made with the third edition in 2005.

NEC has played a part in helping the industry do things differently and better. It has done so by introducing effective project management procedures into the contract itself. These require pro-active management of risk and change, and the day-to-day use of an up-to-date programme. The range of pricing options has given Clients flexibility in the allocation of risk and the ability to share risk and manage it, collaboratively.

The NEC suite has evolved over three decades, embedding consultation responses and user feedback, and reflecting industry development, including new procurement approaches and management techniques such as alliances, management of information (BIM) and supply chain engagement. This feedback and the new procurement approaches formed the driver for the development of the next generation contracts and the launch of NEC4.

There were three key objectives in drafting NEC4:

- provide greater stimulus to good management

- support new approaches to procurement which improve contract management and

- inspire increased use of NEC in new markets and sectors.

It was to be evolution, not revolution.

Some features of NEC4 include:

- a new design build and operate contract to allow flexibility between construction and operational requirements in timing and extent

- a new multi-party alliance contract based upon an integrated risk and reward model

- new forms of subcontract to improve integration of the supply chain.

Further enhancements include:

- finalising cost elements during the contract

- incorporating a party-led dispute avoidance process into the adjudication process

- increasing standardisation between contracts and

- providing enhanced guidance to give greater practical advice to users.

NEC has always been known for its innovative approach to contract management, and this revision continues that approach. No other contract suite has had such a transformative effect on the built environment industry as NEC. It has put the collaborative sharing of risk and reward at the heart of modern procurement. It is also unique in providing a complete, back-to-back procurement solution for all works, services and supplies in any sector and any country.

NEC4 continues to set the benchmark for best practice procurement worldwide.

Peter Higgins BSc (Hons), CEng, FICE
Chair of NEC4 Contract Board

Acknowledgements

The original NEC was designed and drafted by Dr Martin Barnes then of Coopers and Lybrand with the assistance of Professor J. G. Perry then of the University of Birmingham, T. W. Weddell then of Travers Morgan Management, T. H. Nicholson, Consultant to the Institution of Civil Engineers, A. Norman then of the University of Manchester Institute of Science and Technology and P. A. Baird, then Corporate Contracts Consultant, Eskom, South Africa.

This fourth edition of the NEC suite was produced by the Institution of Civil Engineers through its NEC4 Contract Board.

The NEC4 Contract Board is:

P. Higgins, BSc (Hons), CEng, FICE (Chair)
P. T. Cousins, BEng (Tech), DipArb, CEng, MICE, FCIArb
I. Heaphy, BSc (Hons), FRICS, FCIArb, MCInstCES, MACostE
J. N. Hughes-D'Aeth, BA (Hons), MA (Cantab)
S. Rowsell, BSc, CEng, FCIHT, FICE, MCIPS

The NEC4 drafting team consisted of:

M. Garratt, BSc (Hons), MRICS, FCIArb
R. Gerrard, BSc (Hons), FRICS, FCIArb, FCInstCES
R. Hayes, BSc (Hons), MEng, CEng, MICE, MAPM
S. Kings, BSc (Hons), MRICS, MCIPS, PhD
T. Knee-Robinson, BEng (Hons), CEng, MICE, MAPM, MCIHT
J. J. Lofty, MRICS
R. Patterson, BA, MBA, CEng, MICE
B. Trebes, BSc (Hons), MSc, FRICS, FInstCES, FAPM
B. Walker, BSc (Hons), GMICE, ACIArb

Proofreading by:

P. Waterhouse, BEng (Hons), MBA, CEng, FICE, FCIArb, FCInstCES, FCMI

The Institution of Civil Engineers acknowledges the help in preparing the fourth edition given by the NEC4 Contract Board and NEC4 drafting team and the support of the following organisations in releasing their staff:

Anthony Collins Solicitors LLP
Berwin Leighton Paisner LLP
CEMAR
Costain plc
Mott MacDonald Ltd

Amendments

JANUARY 2019

The following amendments have been made to the June 2017 edition.

Page	Clause/location	Amendments
9	28.1	Clause amended
22	63.5	Clause amended
28	90.2	Clause amended
36, 39, 43, 45	50.9	Clause amended
40	63.13	Clause amended
44	11.2(27)	Clause amended
46	W1.1(1)	Clause amended
49	W2.1(1)	Clause amended
53	W3.3(2)	Clause amended
60	X15.6	Clause added
78	Contract Data Part one: General	Preamble amended
84	Contract Data Part one: resolving and avoiding disputes	Optional statement for W3 deleted
93	Contract Data Part one: resolving and avoiding disputes	Optional statement for W3 added

Full details of these amendments can be found at www.neccontract.com.

OCTOBER 2020

The following amendments have been made to the June 2017 edition.

Page	Clause/location	Amendments
55	X7.1	Clause amended
57	X10.7(1)	Clause amended
57	X10.7(2)	Clause amended
62	X22	Clause amended
65	Y(UK)1	Clause amended
78	Contract Data Part One: General	Preamble amended
90	Contract Data Part One: Y(UK)1	Entry amended

Full details of these amendments can be found at www.neccontract.com.

Schedule of Options

MAIN OPTIONS	The strategy for choosing the form of contract starts with a decision between six main Options, one of which must be chosen.
Option A	Priced contract with activity schedule
Option B	Priced contract with bill of quantities
Option C	Target contract with activity schedule
Option D	Target contract with bill of quantities
Option E	Cost reimbursable contract
Option F	Management contract
RESOLVING AND AVOIDING DISPUTES	One of the following procedures for resolving and avoiding disputes must be selected to complete the chosen main Option.
Option W1	Used when adjudication is the method of dispute resolution and the United Kingdom Housing Grants, Construction and Regeneration Act 1996 does not apply
Option W2	Used when adjudication is the method of dispute resolution and the United Kingdom Housing Grants, Construction and Regeneration Act 1996 applies
Option W3	Used when a Dispute Avoidance Board is the method of dispute resolution and the United Kingdom Housing Grants, Construction and Regeneration Act 1996 does not apply
SECONDARY OPTIONS	The following secondary Options should then be considered. It is not necessary to use any of them. Any combination other than those stated may be used.
Option X1	Price adjustment for inflation (used only with Options A, B, C and D)
Option X2	Changes in the law
Option X3	Multiple currencies (used only with Options A and B)
Option X4	Ultimate holding company guarantee
Option X5	Sectional Completion
Option X6	Bonus for early Completion
Option X7	Delay damages
Option X8	Undertakings to the *Client* or Others
Option X9	Transfer of rights
Option X10	Information modelling
Option X11	Termination by the *Client*
Option X12	Multiparty collaboration (not used with Option X20)
Option X13	Performance bond
Option X14	Advanced payment to the *Contractor*
Option X15	The *Contractor's* design
Option X16	Retention (not used with Option F)
Option X17	Low performance damages
Option X18	Limitation of liability
Option X20	Key Performance Indicators (not used with Option X12)
Option X21	Whole life cost
Option X22	Early *Contractor* involvement (used only with Options C and E)

The following Options dealing with national legislation should be included if required.

Option Y(UK)1	Project Bank Account
Option Y(UK)2	The Housing Grants, Construction and Regeneration Act 1996
Option Y(UK)3	The Contracts (Rights of Third Parties) Act 1999
Option Z	*Additional conditions of contract*
Note	Option X19 is not used

Core Clauses

1. GENERAL

Actions **10**

10.1   The Parties, the *Project Manager* and the *Supervisor* shall act as stated in this contract.

10.2   The Parties, the *Project Manager* and the *Supervisor* act in a spirit of mutual trust and co-operation.

Identified and **11**
defined terms

11.1   In these *conditions of contract*, terms identified in the Contract Data are in italics and defined terms have capital initials.

11.2   (1) The Accepted Programme is the programme identified in the Contract Data or is the latest programme accepted by the *Project Manager*. The latest programme accepted by the *Project Manager* supersedes previous Accepted Programmes.

(2) Completion is when the *Contractor* has

- done all the work which the Scope states is to be done by the Completion Date and

- corrected notified Defects which would have prevented the *Client* from using the *works* or Others from doing their work.

If the work which the *Contractor* is to do by the Completion Date is not stated in the Scope, Completion is when the *Contractor* has done all the work necessary for the *Client* to use the *works* and for Others to do their work.

(3) The Completion Date is the *completion date* unless later changed in accordance with the contract.

(4) The Contract Date is the date when the contract came into existence.

(5) A Corrupt Act is

- the offering, promising, giving, accepting or soliciting of an advantage as an inducement for an action which is illegal, unethical or a breach of trust or

- abusing any entrusted power for private gain

in connection with this contract or any other contract with the *Client*. This includes any commission paid as an inducement which was not declared to the *Client* before the Contract Date.

(6) A Defect is

- a part of the *works* which is not in accordance with the Scope or

- a part of the *works* designed by the *Contractor* which is not in accordance with the applicable law or the *Contractor's* design which the *Project Manager* has accepted.

(7) The Defects Certificate is either a list of Defects that the *Supervisor* has notified before the *defects date* which the *Contractor* has not corrected or, if there are no such Defects, a statement that there are none.

(8) The Early Warning Register is a register of matters which are

- listed in the Contract Data for inclusion and

- notified by the *Project Manager* or the *Contractor* as early warning matters.

It includes a description of the matter and the way in which the effects of the matter are to be avoided or reduced.

(9) Equipment is items provided and used by the *Contractor* to Provide the Works and which the Scope does not require the *Contractor* to include in the *works*.

(10) The Fee is the amount calculated by applying the *fee percentage* to the amount of Defined Cost.

(11) A Key Date is the date by which work is to meet the Condition stated. The Key Date is the *key date* stated in the Contract Data and the Condition is the *condition* stated in the Contract Data unless later changed in accordance with the contract.

(12) Others are people or organisations who are not the *Client,* the *Project Manager*, the *Supervisor*, the *Adjudicator* or a member of the Dispute Avoidance Board, the *Contractor* or any employee, Subcontractor or supplier of the *Contractor*.

(13) The Parties are the *Client* and the *Contractor*.

(14) Plant and Materials are items intended to be included in the *works*.

(15) To Provide the Works means to do the work necessary to complete the *works* in accordance with the contract and all incidental work, services and actions which the contract requires.

(16) Scope is information which

- specifies and describes the *works* or

- states any constraints on how the *Contractor* Provides the Works

and is either

- in the documents which the Contract Data states it is in or

- in an instruction given in accordance with the contract.

(17) The Site is the area within the *boundaries of the site* and the volumes above and below it which are affected by work included in the contract.

(18) Site Information is information which

- describes the Site and its surroundings and

- is in the documents which the Contract Data states it is in.

(19) A Subcontractor is a person or organisation who has a contract with the *Contractor* to

- construct or install part of the *works*,

- design all or part of the *works*, except the design of Plant and Materials carried out by the supplier or

- provide a service in the Working Areas which is necessary to Provide the Works, except for the

  – hire of Equipment or
  – supply of people paid for by the *Contractor* according to the time they work.

(20) The Working Areas are the Site and those parts of the *working areas* which are

- necessary for Providing the Works and

- used only for work in the contract

unless later changed in accordance with the contract.

Interpretation and the law	**12**	
	12.1	In the contract, except where the context shows otherwise, words in the singular also mean in the plural and the other way round.
	12.2	The contract is governed by the *law of the contract*.
	12.3	No change to the contract, unless provided for by these *conditions of contract*, has effect unless it has been agreed, confirmed in writing and signed by the Parties.
	12.4	The contract is the entire agreement between the Parties.

Communications	**13**	
	13.1	Each communication which the contract requires is communicated in a form which can be read, copied and recorded. Writing is in the *language of the contract*.
	13.2	If the Scope specifies the use of a communication system, a communication has effect when it is communicated through the communication system specified in the Scope.
		If the Scope does not specify a communication system, a communication has effect when it is received at the last address notified by the recipient for receiving communications or, if none is notified, at the address of the recipient stated in the Contract Data.
	13.3	If the contract requires the *Project Manager*, the *Supervisor* or the *Contractor* to reply to a communication, unless otherwise stated in these *conditions of contract*, they reply within the *period for reply*.
	13.4	The *Project Manager* replies to a communication submitted or resubmitted by the *Contractor* for acceptance. If the reply is not acceptance, the *Project Manager* states the reasons in sufficient detail to enable the *Contractor* to correct the matter. The *Contractor* resubmits the communication within the *period for reply* taking account of these reasons. A reason for withholding acceptance is that more information is needed in order to assess the *Contractor's* submission fully.
	13.5	The *Project Manager* may extend the period for reply to a communication if the *Project Manager* and the *Contractor* agree to the extension before the reply is due. The *Project Manager* informs the *Contractor* of the extension which has been agreed.
	13.6	The *Project Manager* issues certificates to the *Client* and the *Contractor*. The *Supervisor* issues certificates to the *Project Manager,* the *Client* and the *Contractor*.
	13.7	A notification or certificate which the contract requires is communicated separately from other communications.
	13.8	The *Project Manager* may withhold acceptance of a submission by the *Contractor*. Withholding acceptance for a reason stated in these *conditions of contract* is not a compensation event.

The *Project Manager* and the *Supervisor*	**14**	
	14.1	The *Project Manager's* or the *Supervisor's* acceptance of a communication from the *Contractor* or acceptance of the work does not change the *Contractor's* responsibility to Provide the Works or liability for its design.
	14.2	The *Project Manager* and the *Supervisor*, after notifying the *Contractor*, may delegate any of their actions and may cancel any delegation. The notification contains the name of the delegate and details of the actions being delegated or any cancellation of delegation. A reference to an action of the *Project Manager* or the *Supervisor* in the contract includes an action by their delegate. The *Project Manager* and the *Supervisor* may take an action which they have delegated.
	14.3	The *Project Manager* may give an instruction to the *Contractor* which changes the Scope or a Key Date.
	14.4	The *Client* may replace the *Project Manager* or the *Supervisor* after notifying the *Contractor* of the name of the replacement.

CORE CLAUSES

MAIN OPTION CLAUSES

SECONDARY OPTION CLAUSES

COST COMPONENTS

CONTRACT DATA

Early warning	**15**	
	15.1	The *Contractor* and the *Project Manager* give an early warning by notifying the other as soon as either becomes aware of any matter which could

- increase the total of the Prices,

- delay Completion,

- delay meeting a Key Date or

- impair the performance of the *works* in use.

The *Project Manager* or the *Contractor* may give an early warning by notifying the other of any other matter which could increase the *Contractor's* total cost. The *Project Manager* enters early warning matters in the Early Warning Register. Early warning of a matter for which a compensation event has previously been notified is not required.

15.2 The *Project Manager* prepares a first Early Warning Register and issues it to the *Contractor* within one week of the *starting date*. The *Project Manager* instructs the *Contractor* to attend a first early warning meeting within two weeks of the *starting date*.

Later early warning meetings are held

- if either the *Project Manager* or *Contractor* instructs the other to attend an early warning meeting, and, in any case,

- at no longer interval than the interval stated in the Contract Data until Completion of the whole of the *works*.

The *Project Manager* or *Contractor* may instruct other people to attend an early warning meeting if the other agrees.

A Subcontractor attends an early warning meeting if its attendance would assist in deciding the actions to be taken.

15.3 At an early warning meeting, those who attend co-operate in

- making and considering proposals for how the effects of each matter in the Early Warning Register can be avoided or reduced,

- seeking solutions that will bring advantage to all those who will be affected,

- deciding on the actions which will be taken and who, in accordance with the contract, will take them,

- deciding which matters can be removed from the Early Warning Register and

- reviewing actions recorded in the Early Warning Register and deciding if different actions need to be taken and who, in accordance with the contract, will take them.

15.4 The *Project Manager* revises the Early Warning Register to record the decisions made at each early warning meeting and issues the revised Early Warning Register to the *Contractor* within one week of the early warning meeting. If a decision needs a change to the Scope, the *Project Manager* instructs the change at the same time as the revised Early Warning Register is issued.

Contractor's proposals	**16**	
	16.1	The *Contractor* may propose to the *Project Manager* that the Scope provided by the *Client* is changed in order to reduce the amount the *Client* pays to the *Contractor* for Providing the Works. The *Project Manager* consults with the *Client* and the *Contractor* about the change.

16.2 Within four weeks of the *Contractor* making the proposal the *Project Manager*

- accepts the *Contractor's* proposal and issues an instruction changing the Scope,

- informs the *Contractor* that the *Client* is considering the proposal and instructs the *Contractor* to submit a quotation for a proposed instruction to change the Scope or

- informs the *Contractor* that the proposal is not accepted.

The *Project Manager* may give any reason for not accepting the proposal.

16.3 The *Contractor* may submit a proposal for adding an area to the Working Areas to the *Project Manager* for acceptance. A reason for not accepting is that the proposed area is

- not necessary for Providing the Works or

- used for work not in the contract.

Requirements for instructions	**17**

17.1 The *Project Manager* or the *Contractor* notifies the other as soon as either becomes aware of an ambiguity or inconsistency in or between the documents which are part of the contract. The *Project Manager* states how the ambiguity or inconsistency should be resolved.

17.2 The *Project Manager* or the *Contractor* notifies the other as soon as either becomes aware that the Scope includes an illegal or impossible requirement. If the Scope does include an illegal or impossible requirement, the *Project Manager* gives an instruction to change the Scope appropriately.

Corrupt Acts	**18**

18.1 The *Contractor* does not do a Corrupt Act.

18.2 The *Contractor* takes action to stop a Corrupt Act of a Subcontractor or supplier of which it is, or should be, aware.

18.3 The *Contractor* includes equivalent provisions to these in subcontracts and contracts for the supply of Plant and Materials and Equipment.

Prevention	**19**

19.1 If an event occurs which

- stops the *Contractor* completing the whole of the *works* or

- stops the *Contractor* completing the whole of the *works* by the date for planned Completion shown on the Accepted Programme,

and which

- neither Party could prevent and

- an experienced contractor would have judged at the Contract Date to have such a small chance of occurring that it would have been unreasonable to have allowed for it,

the *Project Manager* gives an instruction to the *Contractor* stating how the event is to be dealt with.

CORE CLAUSES

MAIN OPTION CLAUSES

SECONDARY OPTION CLAUSES

COST COMPONENTS

CONTRACT DATA

2. THE *CONTRACTOR'S* MAIN RESPONSIBILITIES

Providing the Works	**20**	
	20.1	The *Contractor* Provides the Works in accordance with the Scope.

The *Contractor's* design	**21**	
	21.1	The *Contractor* designs the parts of the *works* which the Scope states the *Contractor* is to design.
	21.2	The *Contractor* submits the particulars of its design as the Scope requires to the *Project Manager* for acceptance. A reason for not accepting the *Contractor's* design is that it does not comply with either the Scope or the applicable law.
		The *Contractor* does not proceed with the relevant work until the *Project Manager* has accepted its design.
	21.3	The *Contractor* may submit its design for acceptance in parts if the design of each part can be assessed fully.

Using the *Contractor's* design	**22**	
	22.1	The *Client* may use and copy the *Contractor's* design for any purpose connected with construction, use, alteration or demolition of the *works* unless otherwise stated in the Scope and for other purposes as stated in the contract. The *Contractor* obtains from a Subcontractor equivalent rights for the *Client* to use material prepared by the Subcontractor.

Design of Equipment	**23**	
	23.1	The *Contractor* submits particulars of the design of an item of Equipment to the *Project Manager* for acceptance if the *Project Manager* instructs the *Contractor* to. A reason for not accepting is that the design of the item will not allow the *Contractor* to Provide the Works in accordance with

- the Scope,

- the *Contractor's* design which the *Project Manager* has accepted or

- the applicable law.

People	**24**	
	24.1	The *Contractor* either provides each *key person* named to do the job stated in the Contract Data or provides a replacement person who has been accepted by the *Project Manager*.
		The *Contractor* submits the name, relevant qualifications and experience of a proposed replacement person to the *Project Manager* for acceptance. A reason for not accepting the person is that their relevant qualifications and experience are not as good as those of the person who is to be replaced.
	24.2	The *Project Manager* may, having stated the reasons, instruct the *Contractor* to remove a person. The *Contractor* then arranges that, after one day, the person has no further connection with the work included in the contract.

Working with the *Client* and Others	**25**	
	25.1	The *Contractor* co-operates with Others, including in obtaining and providing information which they need in connection with the *works*. The *Contractor* shares the Working Areas with Others as stated in the Scope.
	25.2	The *Client* and the *Contractor* provide services and other things as stated in the Scope. Any cost incurred by the *Client* as a result of the *Contractor* not providing the services and other things which it is to provide is assessed by the *Project Manager* and paid by the *Contractor*.
	25.3	If the *Project Manager* decides that the work does not meet the Condition stated for a Key Date by the date stated and, as a result, the *Client* incurs additional cost either

- in carrying out work or

● by paying an additional amount to Others in carrying out work

on the same project, the additional cost which the *Client* has paid or will incur is paid by the *Contractor*. The *Project Manager* assesses the additional cost within four weeks of the date when the Condition for the Key Date is met. The *Client's* right to recover the additional cost is its only right in these circumstances.

Subcontracting	26	
	26.1	If the *Contractor* subcontracts work, it is responsible for Providing the Works as if it had not subcontracted. The contract applies as if a Subcontractor's employees and equipment were the *Contractor's*.
	26.2	The *Contractor* submits the name of each proposed Subcontractor to the *Project Manager* for acceptance. A reason for not accepting the Subcontractor is that the appointment will not allow the *Contractor* to Provide the Works. The *Contractor* does not appoint a proposed Subcontractor until the *Project Manager* has

● accepted the Subcontractor and, to the extent these *conditions of contract* require,

● accepted the subcontract documents.

26.3 The *Contractor* submits the proposed subcontract documents, except any pricing information, for each subcontract to the *Project Manager* for acceptance unless

● the proposed subcontract is an NEC contract which has not been amended other than in accordance with the *additional conditions of contract* or

● the *Project Manager* has agreed that no submission is required.

A reason for not accepting the subcontract documents is that

● their use will not allow the *Contractor* to Provide the Works or

● they do not include a statement that the parties to the subcontract act in a spirit of mutual trust and co-operation.

Other responsibilities	27	
	27.1	The *Contractor* obtains approval of its design from Others where necessary.
	27.2	The *Contractor* provides access to work being done and to Plant and Materials being stored for the contract for

● the *Project Manager*,

● the *Supervisor* and

● Others as named by the *Project Manager*.

27.3 The *Contractor* obeys an instruction which is in accordance with the contract and is given by the *Project Manager* or the *Supervisor*.

27.4 The *Contractor* acts in accordance with the health and safety requirements stated in the Scope.

Assignment	28	
	28.1	Either Party notifies the other Party if they intend to transfer the benefit of the contract or any rights under it. The *Client* does not transfer a benefit or any rights if the party receiving the benefit or right does not intend to act in a spirit of mutual trust and co-operation.

Disclosure	29	
	29.1	The Parties do not disclose information obtained in connection with the *works* except when necessary to carry out their duties under the contract.
	29.2	The *Contractor* may publicise the *works* only with the *Client's* agreement.

3. TIME

Starting, Completion and Key Dates	30	
	30.1	The *Contractor* does not start work on the Site until the first *access date* and does the work so that Completion is on or before the Completion Date.
	30.2	The *Project Manager* decides the date of Completion and certifies it within one week of the date.
	30.3	The *Contractor* does the work so that the Condition stated for each Key Date is met by the Key Date.

The programme   **31**

31.1   If a programme is not identified in the Contract Data, the *Contractor* submits a first programme to the *Project Manager* for acceptance within the period stated in the Contract Data.

31.2   The *Contractor* shows on each programme submitted for acceptance

- the *starting date*, *access dates*, Key Dates and Completion Date,

- planned Completion,

- the order and timing of the operations which the *Contractor* plans to do in order to Provide the Works,

- the order and timing of the work of the *Client* and Others as last agreed with them by the *Contractor* or, if not so agreed, as stated in the Scope,

- the dates when the *Contractor* plans to meet each Condition stated for the Key Dates and to complete other work needed to allow the *Client* and Others to do their work,

- provisions for

  - float,

  - time risk allowances,

  - health and safety requirements and

  - the procedures set out in the contract,

- the dates when, in order to Provide the Works in accordance with the programme, the *Contractor* will need

  - access to a part of the Site if later than its *access date*,

  - acceptances,

  - Plant and Materials and other things to be provided by the *Client* and

  - information from Others,

- for each operation, a statement of how the *Contractor* plans to do the work identifying the principal Equipment and other resources which will be used and

- other information which the Scope requires the *Contractor* to show on a programme submitted for acceptance.

A programme issued for acceptance is in the form stated in the Scope.

31.3   Within two weeks of the *Contractor* submitting a programme for acceptance, the *Project Manager* notifies the *Contractor* of the acceptance of the programme or the reasons for not accepting it. A reason for not accepting a programme is that

- the *Contractor's* plans which it shows are not practicable,

- it does not show the information which the contract requires,

Sidebar (vertical tabs): CORE CLAUSES · MAIN OPTION CLAUSES · SECONDARY OPTION CLAUSES · COST COMPONENTS · CONTRACT DATA

- it does not represent the *Contractor's* plans realistically or

- it does not comply with the Scope.

If the *Project Manager* does not notify acceptance or non-acceptance within the time allowed, the *Contractor* may notify the *Project Manager* of that failure. If the failure continues for a further one week after the *Contractor's* notification, it is treated as acceptance by the *Project Manager* of the programme.

Revising the programme	**32**	
	32.1	The *Contractor* shows on each revised programme

- the actual progress achieved on each operation and its effect upon the timing of the remaining work,

- how the *Contractor* plans to deal with any delays and to correct notified Defects and

- any other changes which the *Contractor* proposes to make to the Accepted Programme.

32.2 The *Contractor* submits a revised programme to the *Project Manager* for acceptance

- within the *period for reply* after the *Project Manager* has instructed the *Contractor* to,

- when the *Contractor* chooses to and, in any case,

- at no longer interval than the interval stated in the Contract Data from the *starting date* until Completion of the whole of the *works*.

Access to and use of the Site	**33**	
	33.1	The *Client* allows access to and use of each part of the Site to the *Contractor* which is necessary for the work included in the contract. Access and use is allowed on or before the later of its *access date* and the date for access shown on the Accepted Programme.

Instructions to stop or not to start work	**34**	
	34.1	The *Project Manager* may instruct the *Contractor* to stop or not start any work. The *Project Manager* subsequently gives an instruction to the *Contractor* to

- re-start or start the work or

- remove the work from the Scope.

Take over	**35**	
	35.1	The *Client* need not take over the *works* before the Completion Date if the Contract Data states it is not willing to do so. Otherwise the *Client* takes over the *works* not later than two weeks after Completion.
	35.2	The *Client* may use any part of the *works* before Completion has been certified. The *Client* takes over the part of the *works* when it begins to use it except if the use is

- for a reason stated in the Scope or

- to suit the *Contractor's* method of working.

35.3 The *Project Manager* certifies the date upon which the *Client* takes over any part of the *works* and its extent within one week of the date.

Acceleration	**36**	
	36.1	The *Contractor* and the *Project Manager* may propose to the other an acceleration to achieve Completion before the Completion Date. If the *Project Manager* and *Contractor* are prepared to consider the proposed change, the *Project Manager* instructs the *Contractor* to provide a quotation. The instruction states changes to the Key Dates to be included in the quotation. The *Contractor* provides a quotation within three weeks of the instruction to do so. The *Project Manager* replies to the quotation within three weeks. The reply is

- a notification that the quotation is accepted or

- a notification that the quotation is not accepted and that the Completion Dates and Key Dates are not changed.

CORE CLAUSES

MAIN OPTION CLAUSES

SECONDARY OPTION CLAUSES

COST COMPONENTS

CONTRACT DATA

36.2 A quotation for an acceleration comprises proposed changes to the Prices and a revised programme showing the earlier Completion Date and the changed Key Dates. The *Contractor* submits details of the assessment with each quotation.

36.3 When a quotation for an acceleration is accepted, the *Project Manager* changes the Prices, the Completion Date and the Key Dates accordingly and accepts the revised programme.

4. QUALITY MANAGEMENT

Quality management system	**40**	
	40.1	The *Contractor* operates a quality management system which complies with the requirements stated in the Scope.
	40.2	Within the period stated in the Contract Data, the *Contractor* provides the *Project Manager* with a quality policy statement and a quality plan for acceptance. A reason for not accepting a quality policy statement or quality plan is that it does not allow the *Contractor* to Provide the Works.
		If any changes are made to the quality plan, the *Contractor* provides the *Project Manager* with the changed quality plan for acceptance.
	40.3	The *Project Manager* may instruct the *Contractor* to correct a failure to comply with the quality plan. This instruction is not a compensation event.

Tests and inspections	**41**	
	41.1	This clause only applies to tests and inspections required by the Scope or the applicable law.
	41.2	The *Contractor* and the *Client* provide materials, facilities and samples for tests and inspections as stated in the Scope.
	41.3	The *Contractor* and the *Supervisor* informs the other of each of their tests and inspections before the test or inspection starts and afterwards informs the other of the results. The *Contractor* informs the *Supervisor* in time for a test or inspection to be arranged and done before doing work which would obstruct the test or inspection. The *Supervisor* may watch any test done by the *Contractor*.
	41.4	If a test or inspection shows that any work has a Defect, the *Contractor* corrects the Defect and the test or inspection is repeated.
	41.5	The *Supervisor* does tests and inspections without causing unnecessary delay to the work or to a payment which is conditional upon a test or inspection being successful. A payment which is conditional upon a *Supervisor's* test or inspection being successful becomes due at the later of the *defects date* and the end of the last *defect correction period* if

  • the *Supervisor* has not done the test or inspection and

  • the delay to the test or inspection is not the *Contractor's* fault.

	41.6	The *Project Manager* assesses the cost incurred by the *Client* in repeating a test or inspection after a Defect is found. The *Contractor* pays the amount assessed.

Testing and inspection before delivery	**42**	
	42.1	The *Contractor* does not bring to the Working Areas those Plant and Materials which the Scope states are to be tested or inspected before delivery until the *Supervisor* has notified the *Contractor* that they have passed the test or inspection.

Searching for and notifying Defects	**43**	
	43.1	Until the *defects date,* the *Supervisor* may instruct the *Contractor* to search for a Defect. The *Supervisor* gives reasons for the search with the instruction. Searching may include

  • uncovering, dismantling, re-covering and re-erecting work,

  • providing facilities, materials and samples for tests and inspections done by the *Supervisor* and

  • doing tests and inspections which the Scope does not require.

	43.2	Until the *defects date* the *Supervisor* and the *Contractor* notifies the other as soon as they become aware of a Defect.

Correcting Defects	**44**	
	44.1	The *Contractor* corrects a Defect whether or not the *Supervisor* has notified it.
	44.2	The *Contractor* corrects a notified Defect before the end of the *defect correction period*. The *defect correction period* begins at Completion for Defects notified before Completion and when the Defect is notified for other Defects.

44.3 The *Supervisor* issues the Defects Certificate at the *defects date* if there are no notified Defects, or otherwise at the earlier of

- the end of the last *defect correction period* and

- the date when all notified Defects have been corrected.

The *Client's* rights in respect of a Defect which the *Supervisor* has not found or notified are not affected by the issue of the Defects Certificate.

44.4 The *Project Manager* arranges for the *Client* to allow the *Contractor* access to and use of a part of the *works* which has been taken over if it is needed for correcting a Defect. In this case the *defect correction period* begins when the necessary access and use have been provided.

Accepting Defects **45**

45.1 The *Contractor* and the *Project Manager* may propose to the other that the Scope should be changed so that a Defect does not have to be corrected.

45.2 If the *Contractor* and the *Project Manager* are prepared to consider the change, the *Contractor* submits a quotation for reduced Prices or an earlier Completion Date or both to the *Project Manager* for acceptance. If the quotation is accepted, the *Project Manager* changes the Scope, the Prices and the Completion Date accordingly and accepts the revised programme.

Uncorrected **46**
Defects

46.1 If the *Contractor* is given access in order to correct a notified Defect but the Defect is not corrected within its *defect correction period*, the *Project Manager* assesses the cost to the *Client* of having the Defect corrected by other people and the *Contractor* pays this amount. The Scope is treated as having been changed to accept the Defect.

46.2 If the *Contractor* is not given access in order to correct a notified Defect before the *defects date*, the *Project Manager* assesses the cost to the *Contractor* of correcting the Defect and the *Contractor* pays this amount. The Scope is treated as having been changed to accept the Defect.

5. PAYMENT

Assessing the amount due	**50**	
	50.1	The *Project Manager* assesses the amount due at each assessment date. The first assessment date is decided by the *Project Manager* to suit the procedures of the Parties and is not later than the *assessment interval* after the *starting date*. Later assessment dates occur at the end of each *assessment interval* until

- the *Supervisor* issues the Defects Certificate or

- the *Project Manager* issues a termination certificate.

50.2 The *Contractor* submits an application for payment to the *Project Manager* before each assessment date setting out the amount the *Contractor* considers is due at the assessment date. The *Contractor's* application for payment includes details of how the amount has been assessed and is in the form stated in the Scope.

In assessing the amount due, the *Project Manager* considers an application for payment submitted by the *Contractor* before the assessment date.

50.3 If the *Contractor* submits an application for payment before the assessment date, the amount due at the assessment date is

- the Price for Work Done to Date,

- plus other amounts to be paid to the *Contractor*,

- less amounts to be paid by or retained from the *Contractor*.

50.4 If the *Contractor* does not submit an application for payment before the assessment date, the amount due at the assessment date is the lesser of

- the amount the *Project Manager* assesses as due at the assessment date, assessed as though the *Contractor* had submitted an application before the assessment date, and

- the amount due at the previous assessment date.

50.5 If no programme is identified in the Contract Data, one quarter of the Price for Work Done to Date is retained in assessments of the amount due until the *Contractor* has submitted a first programme to the *Project Manager* for acceptance showing the information which the contract requires.

50.6 The *Project Manager* corrects any incorrectly assessed amount due in a later payment certificate.

Payment	**51**	
	51.1	The *Project Manager* certifies a payment within one week of each assessment date. The *Project Manager's* certificate includes details of how the amount due has been assessed. The first payment is the amount due. Other payments are the change in the amount due since the previous assessment. A payment is made by the *Contractor* to the *Client* if the change reduces the amount due. Other payments are made by the *Client* to the *Contractor*. Payments are in the *currency of the contract* unless otherwise stated in the contract.

51.2 Each certified payment is made within three weeks of the assessment date or, if a different period is stated in the Contract Data, within the period stated. If a certified payment is late, or if a payment is late because the *Project Manager* has not issued a certificate which should be issued, interest is paid on the late payment. Interest is assessed from the date by which the late payment should have been made until the date when the late payment is made, and is included in the first assessment after the late payment is made.

51.3 If an amount due is corrected in a later certificate

- in relation to a mistake or a compensation event,

- because a payment was delayed by an unnecessary delay to a test or inspection done by the *Supervisor* or

- following a decision of the *Adjudicator* or the *tribunal*, or a recommendation of the Dispute Avoidance Board,

interest on the correcting amount is paid. Interest is assessed from the date when the incorrect amount was certified until the date when the changed amount is certified and is included in the assessment which includes the changed amount.

51.4 Interest is calculated on a daily basis at the *interest rate* and is compounded annually.

51.5 Any tax which the law requires a Party to pay to the other Party is added to any payment made under the contract.

Defined Cost   52

52.1 All the *Contractor's* costs which are not included in the Defined Cost are treated as included in the Fee. Defined Cost includes only amounts calculated using rates and percentages stated in the Contract Data and other amounts at open market or competitively tendered prices with deductions for all discounts, rebates and taxes which can be recovered.

Final assessment   53

53.1 The *Project Manager* makes an assessment of the final amount due and certifies a final payment, if any is due, no later than

- four weeks after the *Supervisor* issues the Defects Certificate or

- thirteen weeks after the *Project Manager* issues a termination certificate.

The *Project Manager* gives the *Contractor* details of how the amount due has been assessed. The final payment is made within three weeks of the assessment or, if a different period is stated in the Contract Data, within the period stated.

53.2 If the *Project Manager* does not make this assessment within the time allowed, the *Contractor* may issue to the *Client* an assessment of the final amount due, giving details of how the final amount due has been assessed. If the *Client* agrees with this assessment, a final payment is made within three weeks of the assessment or, if a different period is stated in the Contract Data, within the period stated.

53.3 An assessment of the final amount due issued within the time stated in the contract is conclusive evidence of the final amount due under or in connection with the contract unless a Party takes the following actions.

If the contract includes Option W1, a Party

- refers a dispute about the assessment of the final amount due to the *Senior Representatives* within four weeks of the assessment being issued,

- refers any issues not agreed by the *Senior Representatives* to the *Adjudicator* within three weeks of the list of the issues not agreed being produced or when it should have been produced and

- refers to the *tribunal* its dissatisfaction with a decision of the *Adjudicator* as to the final assessment of the amount due within four weeks of the decision being made.

If the contract includes Option W2, a Party

- refers a dispute about the assessment of the final amount due to the *Senior Representatives* or to the *Adjudicator* within four weeks of the assessment being issued,

- refers any issues referred to but not agreed by the *Senior Representatives* to the *Adjudicator* within three weeks of the list of issues not agreed being produced or when it should have been produced and

- refers to the *tribunal* its dissatisfaction with a decision of the *Adjudicator* as to the final assessment of the amount due within four weeks of the decision being made.

If the contract includes Option W3, a Party

- refers a dispute about the assessment of the final amount due to the Dispute Avoidance Board and

- refers to the *tribunal* its dissatisfaction with the recommendation of the Dispute Avoidance Board within four weeks of the recommendation being made.

53.4   The assessment of the final amount due is changed to include

*   any agreement the Parties reach and

*   a decision of the *Adjudicator* or recommendation of the Dispute Avoidance Board which has not been referred to the *tribunal* within four weeks of that decision or recommendation.

A changed assessment becomes conclusive evidence of the final amount due under or in connection with the contract.

6. COMPENSATION EVENTS

Compensation events | 60
60.1 | The following events are compensation events.

(1) The *Project Manager* gives an instruction changing the Scope except

- a change made in order to accept a Defect or

- a change to the Scope provided by the *Contractor* for its design which is made

  - at the *Contractor's* request or

  - in order to comply with the Scope provided by the *Client*.

(2) The *Client* does not allow access to and use of each part of the Site by the later of its *access date* and the date for access shown on the Accepted Programme.

(3) The *Client* does not provide something which it is to provide by the date shown on the Accepted Programme.

(4) The *Project Manager* gives an instruction to stop or not to start any work or to change a Key Date.

(5) The *Client* or Others

- do not work within the times shown on the Accepted Programme,

- do not work within the conditions stated in the Scope or

- carry out work on the Site that is not stated in the Scope.

(6) The *Project Manager* or the *Supervisor* does not reply to a communication from the *Contractor* within the period required by the contract.

(7) The *Project Manager* gives an instruction for dealing with an object of value or of historical or other interest found within the Site.

(8) The *Project Manager* or the *Supervisor* changes a decision which either has previously communicated to the *Contractor*.

(9) The *Project Manager* withholds an acceptance (other than acceptance of a quotation for acceleration or for not correcting a Defect) for a reason not stated in the contract.

(10) The *Supervisor* instructs the *Contractor* to search for a Defect and no Defect is found unless the search is needed only because the *Contractor* gave insufficient notice of doing work obstructing a required test or inspection.

(11) A test or inspection done by the *Supervisor* causes unnecessary delay.

(12) The *Contractor* encounters physical conditions which

- are within the Site,

- are not weather conditions and

- an experienced contractor would have judged at the Contract Date to have such a small chance of occurring that it would have been unreasonable to have allowed for them.

Only the difference between the physical conditions encountered and those for which it would have been reasonable to have allowed is taken into account in assessing a compensation event.

(13) A *weather measurement* is recorded

- within a calendar month,

- before the Completion Date for the whole of the *works* and

- at the place stated in the Contract Data

the value of which, by comparison with the *weather data*, is shown to occur on average less frequently than once in ten years.

Only the difference between the *weather measurement* and the weather which the *weather data* show to occur on average less frequently than once in ten years is taken into account in assessing a compensation event.

(14) An event which is a *Client's* liability stated in these *conditions of contract*.

(15) The *Project Manager* certifies take over of a part of the *works* before both Completion and the Completion Date.

(16) The *Client* does not provide materials, facilities and samples for tests and inspections as stated in the Scope.

(17) The *Project Manager* notifies the *Contractor* of a correction to an assumption which the *Project Manager* stated about a compensation event.

(18) A breach of contract by the *Client* which is not one of the other compensation events in the contract.

(19) An event which

- stops the *Contractor* completing the whole of the *works* or

- stops the *Contractor* completing the whole of the *works* by the date for planned Completion shown on the Accepted Programme,

and which

- neither Party could prevent,

- an experienced contractor would have judged at the Contract Date to have such a small chance of occurring that it would have been unreasonable to have allowed for it and

- is not one of the other compensation events stated in the contract.

(20) The *Project Manager* notifies the *Contractor* that a quotation for a proposed instruction is not accepted.

(21) Additional compensation events stated in Contract Data part one.

60.2 In judging the physical conditions for the purpose of assessing a compensation event, the *Contractor* is assumed to have taken into account

- the Site Information,

- publicly available information referred to in the Site Information,

- information obtainable from a visual inspection of the Site and

- other information which an experienced contractor could reasonably be expected to have or to obtain.

60.3 If there is an ambiguity or inconsistency within the Site Information (including the information referred to in it), the *Contractor* is assumed to have taken into account the physical conditions more favourable to doing the work.

Notifying compensation events **61**

61.1 For a compensation event which arises from the *Project Manager* or the *Supervisor* giving an instruction or notification, issuing a certificate or changing an earlier decision, the *Project Manager* notifies the *Contractor* of the compensation event at the time of that communication.

61.2　The *Project Manager* includes in the notification of a compensation event an instruction to the *Contractor* to submit quotations unless

- the event arises from a fault of the *Contractor* or

- the event has no effect upon Defined Cost, Completion or meeting a Key Date.

61.3　The *Contractor* notifies the *Project Manager* of an event which has happened or which is expected to happen as a compensation event if

- the *Contractor* believes that the event is a compensation event and

- the *Project Manager* has not notified the event to the *Contractor*.

If the *Contractor* does not notify a compensation event within eight weeks of becoming aware that the event has happened, the Prices, the Completion Date or a Key Date are not changed unless the event arises from the *Project Manager* or the *Supervisor* giving an instruction or notification, issuing a certificate or changing an earlier decision.

61.4　The *Project Manager* replies to the *Contractor's* notification of a compensation event within

- one week after the *Contractor's* notification or

- a longer period to which the *Contractor* has agreed.

If the event

- arises from a fault of the *Contractor*,

- has not happened and is not expected to happen,

- has not been notified within the timescales set out in these *conditions of contract*,

- has no effect upon Defined Cost, Completion or meeting a Key Date or

- is not one of the compensation events stated in the contract

the *Project Manager* notifies the *Contractor* that the Prices, the Completion Date and the Key Dates are not to be changed and states the reasons in the notification. Otherwise, the *Project Manager* notifies the *Contractor* that the event is a compensation event and includes in the notification an instruction to the *Contractor* to submit quotations.

If the *Project Manager* fails to reply to the *Contractor's* notification of a compensation event within the time allowed, the *Contractor* may notify the *Project Manager* of that failure. If the failure continues for a further two weeks after the *Contractor's* notification it is treated as acceptance by the *Project Manager* that the event is a compensation event and an instruction to submit quotations.

61.5　If the *Project Manager* decides that the *Contractor* did not give an early warning of the event which an experienced contractor could have given, the *Project Manager* states this in the instruction to the *Contractor* to submit quotations.

61.6　If the effects of a compensation event are too uncertain to be forecast reasonably, the *Project Manager* states assumptions about the compensation event in the instruction to the *Contractor* to submit quotations. Assessment of the event is based on these assumptions. If any of them is later found to have been wrong, the *Project Manager* notifies a correction.

61.7　A compensation event is not notified by the *Project Manager* or the *Contractor* after the issue of the Defects Certificate.

Quotations for　　**62**
compensation　　62.1　After discussing with the *Contractor* different ways of dealing with the compensation event
events　　　　　which are practicable, the *Project Manager* may instruct the *Contractor* to submit alternative quotations. The *Contractor* submits the required quotations to the *Project Manager* and may submit quotations for other methods of dealing with the compensation event which it considers practicable.

CORE CLAUSES

MAIN OPTION CLAUSES

SECONDARY OPTION CLAUSES

COST COMPONENTS

CONTRACT DATA

62.2 Quotations for a compensation event comprise proposed changes to the Prices and any delay to the Completion Date and Key Dates assessed by the *Contractor*. The *Contractor* submits details of the assessment with each quotation. If the programme for remaining work is altered by the compensation event, the *Contractor* includes the alterations to the Accepted Programme in the quotation.

62.3 The *Contractor* submits quotations within three weeks of being instructed to do so by the *Project Manager*. The *Project Manager* replies within two weeks of the submission. The reply is

- a notification of acceptance of the quotation,

- an instruction to submit a revised quotation or

- that the *Project Manager* will be making the assessment.

62.4 The *Project Manager* instructs the *Contractor* to submit a revised quotation only after explaining the reasons for doing so to the *Contractor*. The *Contractor* submits the revised quotation within three weeks of being instructed to do so.

62.5 The *Project Manager* extends the time allowed for

- the *Contractor* to submit quotations for a compensation event or

- the *Project Manager* to reply to a quotation

if the *Project Manager* and the *Contractor* agree to the extension before the submission or reply is due. The *Project Manager* informs the *Contractor* of the extension which has been agreed.

62.6 If the *Project Manager* does not reply to a quotation within the time allowed, the *Contractor* may notify the *Project Manager* of that failure. If the *Contractor* submitted more than one quotation for the compensation event, the notification states which quotation the *Contractor* proposes is to be used. If the failure continues for a further two weeks after the *Contractor's* notification it is treated as acceptance by the *Project Manager* of the quotation.

Assessing compensation events	**63**

63.1 The change to the Prices is assessed as the effect of the compensation event upon

- the actual Defined Cost of the work done by the dividing date,

- the forecast Defined Cost of the work not done by the dividing date and

- the resulting Fee.

For a compensation event that arises from the *Project Manager* or the *Supervisor* giving an instruction or notification, issuing a certificate or changing an earlier decision, the dividing date is the date of that communication.

For other compensation events, the dividing date is the date of the notification of the compensation event.

63.2 The *Project Manager* and the *Contractor* may agree rates or lump sums to assess the change to the Prices.

63.3 If the effect of a compensation event is to reduce the total Defined Cost, the Prices are not reduced unless otherwise stated in these *conditions of contract*.

63.4 If the effect of a compensation event is to reduce the total Defined Cost and the event is

- a change to the Scope other than a change to the Scope provided by the *Client,* which the *Contractor* proposed and the *Project Manager* accepted or

- a correction to an assumption stated by the *Project Manager* for assessing an earlier compensation event

the Prices are reduced.

CORE CLAUSES

MAIN OPTION CLAUSES

SECONDARY OPTION CLAUSES

COST COMPONENTS

CONTRACT DATA

63.5 A delay to the Completion Date is assessed as the length of time that, due to the compensation event, planned Completion is later than planned Completion as shown on the Accepted Programme current at the dividing date.

A delay to a Key Date is assessed as the length of time that, due to the compensation event, the planned date when the Condition stated for a Key Date will be met is later than the date shown on the Accepted Programme current at the dividing date.

The assessment takes into account

- any delay caused by the compensation event already in the Accepted Programme and

- events which have happened between the date of the Accepted Programme and the dividing date.

63.6 The rights of the *Client* and the *Contractor* to changes to the Prices, the Completion Date and the Key Dates are their only rights in respect of a compensation event.

63.7 If the *Project Manager* has stated in the instruction to submit quotations that the *Contractor* did not give an early warning of the event which an experienced contractor could have given, the compensation event is assessed as if the *Contractor* had given the early warning.

63.8 The assessment of the effect of a compensation event includes risk allowances for cost and time for matters which have a significant chance of occurring and are not compensation events.

63.9 The assessment of the effect of a compensation event is based upon the assumptions that the *Contractor* reacts competently and promptly to the event and that any Defined Cost and time due to the event are reasonably incurred.

63.10 A compensation event which is an instruction to change the Scope in order to resolve an ambiguity or inconsistency is assessed as if the Prices, the Completion Date and the Key Dates were for the interpretation most favourable to the Party which did not provide the Scope.

63.11 If a change to the Scope makes the description of the Condition for a Key Date incorrect, the *Project Manager* corrects the description. This correction is taken into account in assessing the compensation event for the change to the Scope.

| **The *Project Manager's* assessments** | 64 | |
| | 64.1 | The *Project Manager* assesses a compensation event |

- if the *Contractor* has not submitted the quotation and details of its assessment within the time allowed,

- if the *Project Manager* decides that the *Contractor* has not assessed the compensation event correctly in the quotation and has not instructed the *Contractor* to submit a revised quotation,

- if, when the *Contractor* submits quotations for the compensation event, it has not submitted a programme or alterations to a programme which the contract requires it to submit or

- if, when the *Contractor* submits quotations for the compensation event, the *Project Manager* has not accepted the *Contractor's* latest programme for one of the reasons stated in the contract.

64.2 The *Project Manager* assesses the programme for the remaining work and uses it in the assessment of a compensation event if

- there is no Accepted Programme,

- the *Contractor* has not submitted a programme or alterations to a programme for acceptance as required by the contract or

- the *Project Manager* has not accepted the *Contractor's* latest programme for one of the reasons stated in the contract.

64.3 The *Project Manager* notifies the *Contractor* of the assessment of a compensation event and gives details of the assessment within the period allowed for the *Contractor's* submission of its quotation for the same compensation event. This period starts when the need for the *Project Manager's* assessment becomes apparent.

64.4 If the *Project Manager* does not assess a compensation event within the time allowed, the *Contractor* may notify the *Project Manager* of that failure. If the *Contractor* submitted more than one quotation for the compensation event, the notification states which quotation the *Contractor* proposes is to be used. If the failure continues for a further two weeks after the *Contractor's* notification it is treated as acceptance by the *Project Manager* of the quotation.

Proposed instructions	**65**	

65.1 The *Project Manager* may instruct the *Contractor* to submit a quotation for a proposed instruction. The *Project Manager* states in the instruction the date by which the proposed instruction may be given. The *Contractor* does not put a proposed instruction into effect.

65.2 The *Contractor* submits quotations for a proposed instruction within three weeks of being instructed to do so by the *Project Manager*. The quotation is assessed as a compensation event. The *Project Manager* replies to the *Contractor's* quotation by the date when the proposed instruction may be given. The reply is

● an instruction to submit a revised quotation including the reasons for doing so,

● the issue of the instruction together with a notification of the instruction as a compensation event and acceptance of the quotation or

● a notification that the quotation is not accepted.

If the *Project Manager* does not reply to the quotation within the time allowed, the quotation is not accepted.

65.3 If the quotation is not accepted, the *Project Manager* may issue the instruction, notify the instruction as a compensation event and instruct the *Contractor* to submit a quotation.

Implementing compensation events	**66**	

66.1 A compensation event is implemented when

● the *Project Manager* notifies acceptance of the *Contractor's* quotation,

● the *Project Manager* notifies the *Contractor* of an assessment made by the *Project Manager* or

● a *Contractor's* quotation is treated as having been accepted by the *Project Manager*.

66.2 When a compensation event is implemented the Prices, the Completion Date and the Key Dates are changed accordingly.

66.3 The assessment of an implemented compensation event is not revised except as stated in these *conditions of contract*.

7. TITLE

The *Client's* title to Plant and Materials	**70**	
	70.1	Whatever title the *Contractor* has to Plant and Materials which are outside the Working Areas passes to the *Client* if the *Supervisor* has marked them as for the contract.
	70.2	Whatever title the *Contractor* has to Plant and Materials passes to the *Client* if they have been brought within the Working Areas. The title to Plant and Materials passes back to the *Contractor* if they are removed from the Working Areas with the *Project Manager's* permission.

Marking Equipment, Plant and Materials outside the Working Areas **71**

71.1 The *Supervisor* marks Equipment, Plant and Materials which are outside the Working Areas if

- the contract identifies them for payment and

- the *Contractor* has prepared them for marking as the Scope requires.

Removing Equipment **72**

72.1 The *Contractor* removes Equipment from the Site when it is no longer needed unless the *Project Manager* allows it to be left in the *works*.

Objects and materials within the Site **73**

73.1 The *Contractor* has no title to an object of value or of historical or other interest within the Site. The *Contractor* informs the *Project Manager* when such an object is found and the *Project Manager* instructs the *Contractor* how to deal with it. The *Contractor* does not move the object without instructions.

73.2 The *Contractor* has title to materials from excavation and demolition unless the Scope states otherwise.

The *Contractor's* use of material **74**

74.1 The *Contractor* has the right to use material provided by the *Client* only to Provide the Works. The *Contractor* may make this right available to a Subcontractor.

8. LIABILITIES AND INSURANCE

Client's liabilities   80

80.1   The following are *Client's* liabilities.

- Claims and proceedings from Others and compensation and costs payable to Others which are due to

  - use or occupation of the Site by the *works* or for the purpose of the *works* which is the unavoidable result of the *works* or

  - negligence, breach of statutory duty or interference with any legal right by the *Client* or by any person employed by or contracted to it except the *Contractor*.

- A fault of the *Client* or any person employed by or contracted to it, except the *Contractor*.

- A fault in the design contained in

  - the Scope provided by the *Client* or

  - an instruction from the *Project Manager* changing the Scope.

- Loss of or damage to Plant and Materials supplied to the *Contractor* by the *Client*, or by Others on the *Client's* behalf, until the *Contractor* has received and accepted them.

- Loss of or damage to the *works*, Plant and Materials due to

  - war, civil war, rebellion, revolution, insurrection, military or usurped power,

  - strikes, riots and civil commotion not confined to the *Contractor's* employees or

  - radioactive contamination.

- Loss of or damage to the parts of the *works* taken over by the *Client*, except loss or damage occurring before the issue of the Defects Certificate which is due to

  - a Defect which existed at take over,

  - an event occurring before take over which was not itself a *Client's* liability or

  - the activities of the *Contractor* on the Site after take over.

- Loss of or damage to the *works* and any Equipment, Plant and Materials retained on the Site by the *Client* after a termination, except loss or damage due to the activities of the *Contractor* on the Site after the termination.

- Loss of or damage to property owned or occupied by the *Client* other than the *works*, unless the loss or damage arises from or in connection with the *Contractor* Providing the Works.

- Additional *Client's* liabilities stated in the Contract Data.

Contractor's   81
liabilities

81.1   The following are *Contractor's* liabilities unless they are stated as being *Client's* liabilities.

- Claims and proceedings from Others and compensation and costs payable to Others which arise from or in connection with the *Contractor* Providing the Works.

- Loss of or damage to the *works*, Plant and Materials and Equipment.

- Loss of or damage to property owned or occupied by the *Client* other than the *works*, which arises from or in connection with the *Contractor* Providing the Works.

- Death or bodily injury to the employees of the *Contractor*.

CORE CLAUSES

MAIN OPTION CLAUSES

SECONDARY OPTION CLAUSES

COST COMPONENTS

CONTRACT DATA

Recovery of costs	**82**	
	82.1	Any cost which the *Client* has paid or will pay as a result of an event for which the *Contractor* is liable is paid by the *Contractor*.
	82.2	Any cost which the *Contractor* has paid or will pay to Others as a result of an event for which the *Client* is liable is paid by the *Client*.
	82.3	The right of a Party to recover these costs is reduced if an event for which it was liable contributed to the costs. The reduction is in proportion to the extent that the event for which that Party is liable contributed, taking into account each Party's responsibilities under the contract.

Insurance cover	**83**	
	83.1	The *Client* provides the insurances which the *Client* is to provide as stated in the Contract Data.
	83.2	The *Contractor* provides the insurances stated in the Insurance Table except any insurance which the *Client* is to provide as stated in the Contract Data. The *Contractor* provides additional insurances as stated in the Contract Data.
	83.3	The insurances in the Insurance Table are in the joint names of the Parties except the fourth insurance stated. The insurances provide cover for events which are the *Contractor's* liability from the *starting date* until the Defects Certificate or a termination certificate has been issued.

INSURANCE TABLE	
INSURANCE AGAINST	**MINIMUM AMOUNT OF COVER**
Loss of or damage to the *works*, Plant and Materials	The replacement cost, including the amount stated in the Contract Data for the replacement of any Plant and Materials provided by the *Client*
Loss of or damage to Equipment	The replacement cost
Loss of or damage to property (except the *works*, Plant and Materials and Equipment) and liability for bodily injury to or death of a person (not an employee of the *Contractor*) arising from or in connection with the *Contractor* Providing the Works	The amount stated in the Contract Data for any one event with cross liability so that the insurance applies to the Parties separately
Death of or bodily injury to employees of the *Contractor* arising out of and in the course of their employment in connection with the contract	The greater of the amount required by the applicable law and the amount stated in the Contract Data for any one event

Insurance policies	**84**	
	84.1	Before the *starting date* and on each renewal of the insurance policy until the *defects date*, the *Contractor* submits to the *Project Manager* for acceptance certificates which state that the insurance required by the contract is in force. The certificates are signed by the *Contractor's* insurer or insurance broker. The *Project Manager* accepts the certificates if the insurance complies with the contract and if the insurer's commercial position is strong enough to carry the insured liabilities.
	84.2	Insurance policies include a waiver by the insurers of their subrogation rights against the Parties and the directors and other employees of every insured except where there is fraud.
	84.3	The Parties comply with the terms and conditions of the insurance policies to which they are a party.

If the *Contractor* does not insure	**85**	
	85.1	The *Client* may insure an event or liability which the contract requires the *Contractor* to insure if the *Contractor* does not submit a required certificate. The cost of this insurance to the *Client* is paid by the *Contractor*.

Insurance by the Client   86

86.1   The *Project Manager* submits certificates for insurance provided by the *Client* to the *Contractor* for acceptance before the *starting date* and afterwards as the *Contractor* instructs. The *Contractor* accepts the certificates if the insurance complies with the contract and if the insurer's commercial position is strong enough to carry the insured liabilities.

86.2   The *Contractor's* acceptance of an insurance certificate provided by the *Client* does not change the responsibility of the *Client* to provide the insurances stated in the Contract Data.

86.3   The *Contractor* may insure an event or liability which the contract requires the *Client* to insure if the *Client* does not submit a required certificate. The cost of this insurance to the *Contractor* is paid by the *Client*.

CORE CLAUSES

MAIN OPTION CLAUSES

SECONDARY OPTION CLAUSES

COST COMPONENTS

CONTRACT DATA

9. TERMINATION

| Termination | 90 |
| | |

90.1 If either Party wishes to terminate the *Contractor's* obligation to Provide the Works it notifies the *Project Manager* and the other Party giving details of the reason for terminating. The *Project Manager* issues a termination certificate promptly if the reason complies with the contract.

90.2 A Party may terminate for a reason identified in the Termination Table. The procedures followed and the amounts due on termination are in accordance with the Termination Table.

TERMINATION TABLE			
TERMINATING PARTY	**REASON**	**PROCEDURE**	**AMOUNT DUE**
The *Client*	R1–R15, R18 or R22	P1, P2 and P3	A1 and A3
	R17, R20 or R21	P1 and P4	A1 and A2
The *Contractor*	R1–R10, R16 or R19	P1 and P4	A1, A2 and A4
	R17 or R20	P1 and P4	A1 and A2

90.3 The procedures for termination are implemented immediately after the *Project Manager* has issued a termination certificate.

If the *Client* terminates for one of reasons R1 to R15, R18 or R22 and a certified payment has not been made at the date of the termination certificate, the *Client* need not make the certified payment unless these *conditions of contract* state otherwise.

90.4 After a termination certificate has been issued, the *Contractor* does no further work necessary to Provide the Works.

| Reasons for termination | 91 |
| | |

91.1 Either Party may terminate if the other Party has done one of the following or its equivalent.

- If the other Party is an individual and has

  - presented an application for bankruptcy (R1),

  - had a bankruptcy order made against it (R2),

  - had a receiver appointed over its assets (R3) or

  - made an arrangement with its creditors (R4).

- If the other Party is a company or partnership and has

  - had a winding-up order made against it (R5),

  - had a provisional liquidator appointed to it (R6),

  - passed a resolution for winding-up (other than in order to amalgamate or reconstruct) (R7),

  - had an administration order made against it or had an administrator appointed over it (R8),

  - had a receiver, receiver and manager, or administrative receiver appointed over the whole or a substantial part of its undertaking or assets (R9) or

  - made an arrangement with its creditors (R10).

91.2 The *Client* may terminate if the *Project Manager* has notified that the *Contractor* has not put one of the following defaults right within four weeks of the date when the *Project Manager* notified the *Contractor* of the default.

- Substantially failed to comply with its obligations (R11).

- Not provided a bond or guarantee which the contract requires (R12).

- Appointed a Subcontractor for substantial work before the *Project Manager* has accepted the Subcontractor (R13).

91.3 The *Client* may terminate if the *Project Manager* has notified that the *Contractor* has not stopped one of the following defaults within four weeks of the date when the *Project Manager* notified the *Contractor* of the default.

- Substantially hindered the *Client* or Others (R14).

- Substantially broken a health or safety regulation (R15).

91.4 The *Contractor* may terminate if the *Client* has not paid an amount due under the contract within thirteen weeks of the date that the *Contractor* should have been paid (R16).

91.5 Either Party may terminate if the Parties have been released under the law from further performance of the whole of the contract (R17).

91.6 If the *Project Manager* has instructed the *Contractor* to stop or not to start any substantial work or all work and an instruction allowing the work to re-start or start or removing work from the Scope has not been given within thirteen weeks,

- the *Client* may terminate if the instruction was due to a default by the *Contractor* (R18),

- the *Contractor* may terminate if the instruction was due to a default by the *Client* (R19) and

- either Party may terminate if the instruction was due to any other reason (R20).

91.7 The *Client* may terminate if an event occurs which

- stops the *Contractor* completing the whole of the *works* or

- stops the *Contractor* completing the whole of the *works* by the date for planned Completion shown on the Accepted Programme and is forecast to delay Completion of the whole of the *works* by more than thirteen weeks,

and which

- neither Party could prevent and

- an experienced contractor would have judged at the Contract Date to have such a small chance of occurring that it would have been unreasonable to have allowed for it (R21).

91.8 The *Client* may terminate if the *Contractor* does a Corrupt Act, unless it was done by a Subcontractor or supplier and the *Contractor*

- was not and should not have been aware of the Corrupt Act or

- informed the *Project Manager* of the Corrupt Act and took action to stop it as soon as the *Contractor* became aware of it (R22).

Procedures on termination | 92

92.1 On termination, the *Client* may complete the *works* and may use any Plant and Materials to which it has title (P1).

92.2 The procedure on termination also includes one or more of the following as set out in the Termination Table.

P2 The *Client* may instruct the *Contractor* to leave the Site, remove any Equipment, Plant and Materials from the Site and assign the benefit of any subcontract or other contract related to performance of the contract to the *Client*.

P3   The *Client* may use any Equipment to which the *Contractor* has title to complete the *works*. The *Contractor* promptly removes the Equipment from Site when the *Project Manager* informs the *Contractor* that the *Client* no longer requires it to complete the *works*.

P4   The *Contractor* leaves the Working Areas and removes the Equipment.

Payment on termination	**93**

93.1   The amount due on termination includes (A1)

- an amount due assessed as for normal payments,

- the Defined Cost for Plant and Materials

   – within the Working Areas or

   – to which the *Client* has title and of which the *Contractor* has to accept delivery,

- other Defined Cost reasonably incurred in expectation of completing the whole of the *works*,

- any amounts retained by the *Client* and

- a deduction of any un-repaid balance of an advanced payment.

93.2   The amount due on termination also includes one or more of the following as set out in the Termination Table.

A2   The forecast Defined Cost of removing Equipment.

A3   A deduction of the forecast of the additional cost to the *Client* of completing the whole of the *works*.

A4   The *fee percentage* applied to

   – for Options A, B, C and D, any excess of the total of the Prices at the Contract Date over the Price for Work Done to Date or

   – for Options E and F, any excess of the first forecast of the Defined Cost for the *works* over the Price for Work Done to Date less the Fee.

Main Option Clauses

OPTION A: PRICED CONTRACT WITH ACTIVITY SCHEDULE

Identified and defined terms	**11** 11.2	(21) The Activity Schedule is the *activity schedule* unless later changed in accordance with these *conditions of contract*.

(23) Defined Cost is the cost of the components in the Short Schedule of Cost Components.

(28) The People Rates are the *people rates* unless later changed in accordance with the contract.

(29) The Price for Work Done to Date is the total of the Prices for

- each group of completed activities and

- each completed activity which is not in a group.

A completed activity is one without notified Defects the correction of which will delay following work.

(32) The Prices are the lump sum prices for each of the activities on the Activity Schedule unless later changed in accordance with the contract.

The programme	**31** 31.4	The *Contractor* provides information which shows how each activity on the Activity Schedule relates to the operations on each programme submitted for acceptance.

The Activity Schedule	**55** 55.1	Information in the Activity Schedule is not Scope or Site Information. If the activities on the Activity Schedule do not relate to the Scope, the *Contractor* corrects the Activity Schedule.
	55.3	If the *Contractor*

- changes a planned method of working at its discretion so that the activities on the Activity Schedule do not relate to the operations on the Accepted Programme or

- corrects the Activity Schedule so that the activities on the Activity Schedule relate to the Scope

the *Contractor* submits a revision of the Activity Schedule to the *Project Manager* for acceptance.

	55.4	A reason for not accepting a revision of the Activity Schedule is that

- it does not relate to the operations on the Accepted Programme,

- any changed Prices are not reasonably distributed between the activities which are not completed or

- the total of the Prices is changed.

Assessing compensation events	**63** 63.12	If the effect of a compensation event is to reduce the total Defined Cost and the event is a change to the Scope provided by the *Client,* which the *Contractor* proposed and the *Project Manager* accepted, the Prices are reduced by an amount calculated by multiplying the assessed effect of the compensation event by the *value engineering percentage*.
	63.14	Assessments for changed Prices for compensation events are in the form of changes to the Activity Schedule.

63.16 If, when assessing a compensation event the People Rates do not include a rate for a category of person required, the *Project Manager* and *Contractor* may agree a new rate. If they do not agree the *Project Manager* assesses the rate based on the People Rates. The agreed or assessed rate becomes the People Rate for that category of person.

Payment on   **93**
termination   93.3   The amount due on termination is assessed without taking grouping of activities into account.

OPTION B: PRICED CONTRACT WITH BILL OF QUANTITIES

Identified and defined terms	**11** 11.2	(22) The Bill of Quantities is the *bill of quantities* unless later changed in accordance with these *conditions of contract*.

(23) Defined Cost is the cost of the components in the Short Schedule of Cost Components.

(28) The People Rates are the *people rates* unless later changed in accordance with the contract.

(30) The Price for Work Done to Date is the total of

* the quantity of the work which the *Contractor* has completed for each item in the Bill of Quantities multiplied by the rate and

* a proportion of each lump sum which is the proportion of the work covered by the item which the *Contractor* has completed.

Completed work is work which is without notified Defects the correction of which will delay following work.

(33) The Prices are the lump sums and the amounts obtained by multiplying the rates by the quantities for the items in the Bill of Quantities.

The Bill of Quantities	**56** 56.1	Information in the Bill of Quantities is not Scope or Site Information.

Compensation events	**60** 60.4	A difference between the final total quantity of work done and the quantity stated for an item in the Bill of Quantities is a compensation event if

* the difference does not result from a change to the Scope,

* the difference causes the Defined Cost per unit of quantity to change and

* the rate in the Bill of Quantities for the item multiplied by the final total quantity of work done is more than 0.5% of the total of the Prices at the Contract Date.

If the Defined Cost per unit of quantity is reduced, the affected rate is reduced.

60.5 A difference between the final total quantity of work done and the quantity for an item stated in the Bill of Quantities which delays Completion or the meeting of the Condition stated for a Key Date is a compensation event.

60.6 The *Project Manager* gives an instruction to correct a mistake in the Bill of Quantities which is

* a departure from the rules for item descriptions or division of the work into items in the *method of measurement* or

* due to an ambiguity or inconsistency.

Each such correction is a compensation event which may lead to reduced Prices.

60.7 In assessing a compensation event which results from a correction of an inconsistency between the Bill of Quantities and another document, the *Contractor* is assumed to have taken the Bill of Quantities as correct.

Assessing compensation events	**63** 63.12	If the effect of a compensation event is to reduce the total Defined Cost and the event is a change to the Scope provided by the *Client,* which the *Contractor* proposed and the *Project Manager* accepted, the Prices are reduced by an amount calculated by multiplying the assessed value of the compensation event by the *value engineering percentage*.

CORE CLAUSES

MAIN OPTION CLAUSES

SECONDARY OPTION CLAUSES

COST COMPONENTS

CONTRACT DATA

63.15 Assessments for changed Prices for compensation events are in the form of changes to the Bill of Quantities.

For the whole or a part of a compensation event for work not yet done and for which there is an item in the Bill of Quantities, the changes are

- a changed rate,

- a changed quantity or

- a changed lump sum.

For the whole or a part of a compensation event for work not yet done and for which there is no item in the Bill of Quantities, the change is a new priced item which, unless the *Project Manager* and the *Contractor* agree otherwise, is compiled in accordance with the *method of measurement*.

For the whole or a part of a compensation event for work already done, the change is a new lump sum item.

63.16 If, when assessing a compensation event the People Rates do not include a rate for a category of person required, the *Project Manager* and *Contractor* may agree a new rate. If they do not agree the *Project Manager* assesses the rate based on the People Rates. The agreed or assessed rate becomes the People Rate for that category of person.

OPTION C: TARGET CONTRACT WITH ACTIVITY SCHEDULE

Identified and defined terms	11	
	11.2	(21) The Activity Schedule is the *activity schedule* unless later changed in accordance with these *conditions of contract*.

(24) Defined Cost is the cost of the components in the Schedule of Cost Components less Disallowed Cost.

(26) Disallowed Cost is cost which

- is not justified by the *Contractor's* accounts and records,

- should not have been paid to a Subcontractor or supplier in accordance with its contract,

- was incurred only because the *Contractor* did not

  – follow an acceptance or procurement procedure stated in the Scope,

  – give an early warning which the contract required it to give or

  – give notification to the *Project Manager* of the preparation for and conduct of an adjudication or proceedings of a tribunal between the *Contractor* and a Subcontractor or supplier

and the cost of

- correcting Defects after Completion,

- correcting Defects caused by the *Contractor* not complying with a constraint on how it is to Provide the Works stated in the Scope,

- Plant and Materials not used to Provide the Works (after allowing for reasonable wastage) unless resulting from a change to the Scope,

- resources not used to Provide the Works (after allowing for reasonable availability and utilisation) or not taken away from the Working Areas when the *Project Manager* requested and

- preparation for and conduct of an adjudication, payments to a member of the Dispute Avoidance Board or proceedings of the *tribunal* between the Parties.

(31) The Price for Work Done to Date is the total Defined Cost which the *Project Manager* forecasts will have been paid by the *Contractor* before the next assessment date plus the Fee.

(32) The Prices are the lump sum prices for each of the activities on the Activity Schedule unless later changed in accordance with the contract.

Providing the Works	20	
	20.3	The *Contractor* advises the *Project Manager* on the practical implications of the design of the *works* and on subcontracting arrangements.
	20.4	The *Contractor* prepares forecasts of the total Defined Cost for the whole of the *works* in consultation with the *Project Manager* and submits them to the *Project Manager*. Forecasts are prepared at the intervals stated in the Contract Data from the *starting date* until Completion of the whole of the *works*. An explanation of the changes made since the previous forecast is submitted with each forecast.

Subcontracting	26	
	26.4	The *Contractor* submits the pricing information in the proposed subcontract documents for each subcontract to the *Project Manager* unless the *Project Manager* has agreed that no submission is required.

CORE CLAUSES

MAIN OPTION CLAUSES

SECONDARY OPTION CLAUSES

COST COMPONENTS

CONTRACT DATA

Tests and inspections	41 41.7	When the *Project Manager* assesses the cost incurred by the *Client* in repeating a test or inspection after a Defect is found, the *Project Manager* does not include the *Contractor's* cost of carrying out the repeat test or inspection.

Assessing the amount due

50

50.7 Payments of Defined Cost made by the *Contractor* in a currency other than the *currency of the contract* are included in the amount due as payments to be made to it in the same currency. Such payments are converted to the *currency of the contract* in order to calculate the Fee and any *Contractor's* share using the *exchange rates*.

50.9 The *Contractor* notifies the *Project Manager* when the Defined Cost for a part of the *works* has been finalised, and makes available for inspection the records necessary to demonstrate that it has been correctly assessed. The *Project Manager* reviews the records made available, and no later than thirteen weeks after the *Contractor's* notification

- accepts that part of Defined Cost as correct,

- notifies the *Contractor* that further records are needed or

- notifies the *Contractor* of errors in its assessment.

The *Contractor* provides any further records requested or advises the correction of the errors in its assessment within four weeks of the *Project Manager's* notification. The *Project Manager* reviews the records provided, and within four weeks

- accepts that part of Defined Cost as correct or

- notifies the *Contractor* of the correct assessment of that part of Defined Cost.

If the *Project Manager* does not notify a decision on that part of Defined Cost within the time stated, the *Contractor's* assessment is treated as correct.

Defined Cost

52

52.2 The *Contractor* keeps these records

- accounts of payments of Defined Cost,

- proof that the payments have been made,

- communications about and assessments of compensation events for Subcontractors and

- other records as stated in the Scope.

52.4 The *Contractor* allows the *Project Manager* to inspect at any time within working hours the accounts and records which it is required to keep.

The *Contractor's* share

54

54.1 The *Project Manager* assesses the *Contractor's* share of the difference between the total of the Prices and the Price for Work Done to Date. The difference is divided into increments falling within each of the *share ranges*. The limits of a *share range* are the Price for Work Done to Date divided by the total of the Prices, expressed as a percentage. The *Contractor's* share equals the sum of the products of the increment within each *share range* and the corresponding *Contractor's share percentage*.

54.2 If the Price for Work Done to Date is less than the total of the Prices, the *Contractor* is paid its share of the saving. If the Price for Work Done to Date is greater than the total of the Prices, the *Contractor* pays its share of the excess.

54.3 The *Project Manager* makes a preliminary assessment of the *Contractor's* share at Completion of the whole of the *works* using forecasts of the final Price for Work Done to Date and the final total of the Prices. This share is included in the amount due following Completion of the whole of the *works*.

54.4 The *Project Manager* makes a final assessment of the *Contractor's* share using the final Price for Work Done to Date and the final total of the Prices. This share is included in the final amount due.

The Activity Schedule	**55**	
	55.2	Information in the Activity Schedule is not Scope or Site Information.

Assessing compensation events	**63**	
	63.13	If the effect of a compensation event is to reduce the total Defined Cost and the event is a change to the Scope provided by the *Client,* which the *Contractor* proposed and the *Project Manager* accepted, the Prices are not reduced.
	63.14	Assessments for changed Prices for compensation events are in the form of changes to the Activity Schedule.

Payment on termination	**93**	
	93.4	If there is a termination, the *Project Manager* assesses the *Contractor's* share after certifying termination. The assessment uses as the Price for Work Done to Date the total of the Defined Cost which the *Contractor* has paid and which it is committed to pay for work done before termination, and uses as the total of the Prices

- the lump sum price for each activity which has been completed and

- a proportion of the lump sum price for each incomplete activity which is the proportion of the work in the activity which has been completed.

	93.6	The *Project Manager's* assessment of the *Contractor's* share is added to the amount due to the *Contractor* on termination if there has been a saving or deducted if there has been an excess.

CORE CLAUSES

MAIN OPTION CLAUSES

SECONDARY OPTION CLAUSES

COST COMPONENTS

CONTRACT DATA

OPTION D: TARGET CONTRACT WITH BILL OF QUANTITIES

Identified and defined terms	11 11.2	(22) The Bill of Quantities is the *bill of quantities* unless later changed in accordance with these *conditions of contract*.

(24) Defined Cost is the cost of the components in the Schedule of Cost Components less Disallowed Cost.

(26) Disallowed Cost is cost which

- is not justified by the *Contractor's* accounts and records,

- should not have been paid to a Subcontractor or supplier in accordance with its contract,

- was incurred only because the *Contractor* did not

  – follow an acceptance or procurement procedure stated in the Scope,

  – give an early warning which the contract required it to give or

  – give notification to the *Project Manager* of the preparation for and conduct of an adjudication or proceedings of a tribunal between the *Contractor* and a Subcontractor or supplier

and the cost of

- correcting Defects after Completion,

- correcting Defects caused by the *Contractor* not complying with a constraint on how it is to Provide the Works stated in the Scope,

- Plant and Materials not used to Provide the Works (after allowing for reasonable wastage) unless resulting from a change to the Scope,

- resources not used to Provide the Works (after allowing for reasonable availability and utilisation) or not taken away from the Working Areas when the *Project Manager* requested and

- preparation for and conduct of an adjudication, or payments to a member of the Dispute Avoidance Board or proceedings of the *tribunal* between the Parties.

(31) The Price for Work Done to Date is the total Defined Cost which the *Project Manager* forecasts will have been paid by the *Contractor* before the next assessment date plus the Fee.

(33) The Prices are the lump sums and the amounts obtained by multiplying the rates by the quantities for the items in the Bill of Quantities.

(35) The Total of the Prices is the total of

- the quantity of the work which the *Contractor* has completed for each item in the Bill of Quantities multiplied by the rate and

- a proportion of each lump sum which is the proportion of the work covered by the item which the *Contractor* has completed.

Completed work is work which is without notified Defects the correction of which will delay following work.

Providing the Works	20 20.3	The *Contractor* advises the *Project Manager* on the practical implications of the design of the *works* and on subcontracting arrangements.

20.4 The *Contractor* prepares forecasts of the total Defined Cost for the whole of the *works* in consultation with the *Project Manager* and submits them to the *Project Manager*. Forecasts are prepared at the intervals stated in the Contract Data from the *starting date* until Completion of the whole of the *works*. An explanation of the changes made since the previous forecast is submitted with each forecast.

Subcontracting   **26**

26.4 The *Contractor* submits the pricing information in the proposed subcontract documents for each subcontract to the *Project Manager* unless the *Project Manager* has agreed that no submission is required.

Tests and   **41**
inspections

41.7 When the *Project Manager* assesses the cost incurred by the *Client* in repeating a test or inspection after a Defect is found, the *Project Manager* does not include the *Contractor's* cost of carrying out the repeat test or inspection.

Assessing the   **50**
amount due

50.7 Payments of Defined Cost made by the *Contractor* in a currency other than the *currency of the contract* are included in the amount due as payments to be made to it in the same currency. Such payments are converted to the *currency of the contract* in order to calculate the Fee and any *Contractor's* share using the *exchange rates*.

50.9 The *Contractor* notifies the *Project Manager* when the Defined Cost for a part of the *works* has been finalised, and makes available for inspection the records necessary to demonstrate that it has been correctly assessed. The *Project Manager* reviews the records made available, and no later than thirteen weeks after the *Contractor's* notification

- accepts that part of Defined Cost as correct,

- notifies the *Contractor* that further records are needed or

- notifies the *Contractor* of errors in its assessment.

The *Contractor* provides any further records requested or advises the correction of the errors in its assessment within four weeks of the *Project Manager's* notification. The *Project Manager* reviews the records provided, and within four weeks

- accepts that part of Defined Cost as correct or

- notifies the *Contractor* of the correct assessment of that part of Defined Cost.

If the *Project Manager* does not notify a decision on that part of Defined Cost within the time stated, the *Contractor's* assessment is treated as correct.

Defined Cost   **52**

52.2 The *Contractor* keeps these records

- accounts of payments of Defined Cost,

- proof that the payments have been made,

- communications about and assessments of compensation events for Subcontractors and

- other records as stated in the Scope.

52.4 The *Contractor* allows the *Project Manager* to inspect at any time within working hours the accounts and records which it is required to keep.

The *Contractor's*   **54**
share

54.5 The *Project Manager* assesses the *Contractor's* share of the difference between the Total of the Prices and the Price for Work Done to Date. The difference is divided into increments falling within each of the *share ranges*. The limits of a *share range* are the Price for Work Done to Date divided by the Total of the Prices, expressed as a percentage. The *Contractor's* share equals the sum of the products of the increment within each *share range* and the corresponding *Contractor's share percentage*.

54.6   If the Price for Work Done to Date is less than the Total of the Prices, the *Contractor* is paid its share of the saving. If the Price for Work Done to Date is greater than the Total of the Prices, the *Contractor* pays its share of the excess.

54.7   The *Project Manager* makes a preliminary assessment of the *Contractor's* share at Completion of the whole of the *works* using forecasts of the final Price for Work Done to Date and the final Total of the Prices. This share is included in the amount due following Completion of the whole of the *works*.

54.8   The *Project Manager* makes a final assessment of the *Contractor's* share using the final Price for Work Done to Date and the final Total of the Prices. This share is included in the final amount due.

The Bill of Quantities	**56**
	56.1 Information in the Bill of Quantities is not Scope or Site Information.

Compensation events   **60**

60.4   A difference between the final total quantity of work done and the quantity stated for an item in the Bill of Quantities is a compensation event if

- the difference does not result from a change to the Scope,

- the difference causes the Defined Cost per unit of quantity to change and

- the rate in the Bill of Quantities for the item multiplied by the final total quantity of work done is more than 0.5% of the total of the Prices at the Contract Date.

If the Defined Cost per unit of quantity is reduced, the affected rate is reduced.

60.5   A difference between the final total quantity of work done and the quantity for an item stated in the Bill of Quantities which delays Completion or the meeting of the Condition stated for a Key Date is a compensation event.

60.6   The *Project Manager* gives an instruction to correct a mistake in the Bill of Quantities which is

- a departure from the rules for item descriptions and or division of the work into items in the *method of measurement* or

- due to an ambiguity or inconsistency.

Each such correction is a compensation event which may lead to reduced Prices.

60.7   In assessing a compensation event which results from a correction of an inconsistency between the Bill of Quantities and another document, the *Contractor* is assumed to have taken the Bill of Quantities as correct.

Assessing compensation events   **63**

63.13   If the effect of a compensation event is to reduce the total Defined Cost and the event is a change to the Scope provided by the *Client*, which the *Contractor* proposed and the *Project Manager* accepted, the Prices are not reduced.

63.15   Assessments for changed Prices for compensation events are in the form of changes to the Bill of Quantities.

For the whole or a part of a compensation event for work not yet done and for which there is an item in the Bill of Quantities, the changes are

- a changed rate,

- a changed quantity or

- a changed lump sum.

For the whole or a part of a compensation event for work not yet done and for which there is no item in the Bill of Quantities, the change is a new priced item which, unless the *Project Manager* and the *Contractor* agree otherwise, is compiled in accordance with the *method of measurement*.

For the whole or a part of a compensation event for work already done, the change is a new lump sum item.

Payment on termination	**93**	
	93.5	If there is a termination, the *Project Manager* assesses the *Contractor's* share after certifying termination. The assessment uses, as the Price for Work Done to Date, the total of the Defined Cost which the *Contractor* has paid and which it is committed to pay for work done before termination.
	93.6	The *Project Manager's* assessment of the *Contractor's* share is added to the amounts due to the *Contractor* on termination if there has been a saving or deducted if there has been an excess.

CORE CLAUSES

MAIN OPTION CLAUSES

SECONDARY OPTION CLAUSES

COST COMPONENTS

CONTRACT DATA

OPTION E: COST REIMBURSABLE CONTRACT

Identified and defined terms	**11** 11.2	(24) Defined Cost is the cost of the components in the Schedule of Cost Components less Disallowed Cost.

(26) Disallowed Cost is cost which

- is not justified by the *Contractor's* accounts and records,

- should not have been paid to a Subcontractor or supplier in accordance with its contract,

- was incurred only because the *Contractor* did not

  – follow an acceptance or procurement procedure stated in the Scope,

  – give an early warning which the contract required it to give or

  – give notification to the *Project Manager* of the preparation for and conduct of an adjudication or proceedings of a *tribunal* between the *Contractor* and a Subcontractor or supplier

and the cost of

- correcting Defects after Completion,

- correcting Defects caused by the *Contractor* not complying with a constraint on how it is to Provide the Works stated in the Scope,

- Plant and Materials not used to Provide the Works (after allowing for reasonable wastage) unless resulting from a change to the Scope,

- resources not used to Provide the Works (after allowing for reasonable availability and utilisation) or not taken away from the Working Areas when the *Project Manager* requested and

- preparation for and conduct of an adjudication, or payments to a member of the Dispute Avoidance Board or proceedings of the tribunal between the Parties.

(31) The Price for Work Done to Date is the total Defined Cost which the *Project Manager* forecasts will have been paid by the *Contractor* before the next assessment date plus the Fee.

(34) The Prices are the forecast of the total Defined Cost for the whole of the *works* plus the Fee.

Providing the Works	**20** 20.3	The *Contractor* advises the *Project Manager* on the practical implications of the design of the *works* and on subcontracting arrangements.
	20.4	The *Contractor* prepares forecasts of the total Defined Cost for the whole of the *works* in consultation with the *Project Manager* and submits them to the *Project Manager*. Forecasts are prepared at the intervals stated in the Contract Data from the *starting date* until Completion of the whole of the *works*. An explanation of the changes made since the previous forecast is submitted with each forecast.

Subcontracting	**26** 26.4	The *Contractor* submits the pricing information in the proposed subcontract documents for each subcontract to the *Project Manager* unless the *Project Manager* has agreed that no submission is required.

Tests and inspections	**41** 41.7	When the *Project Manager* assesses the cost incurred by the *Client* in repeating a test or inspection after a Defect is found, the *Project Manager* does not include the *Contractor's* cost of carrying out the repeat test or inspection.

Assessing the amount due	**50**	
	50.8	Payments of Defined Cost made by the *Contractor* in a currency other than the *currency of the contract* are included in the amount due as payments to be made to it in the same currency. Such payments are converted to the *currency of the contract* in order to calculate the Fee using the *exchange rates*.

50.9 The *Contractor* notifies the *Project Manager* when the Defined Cost for a part of the *works* has been finalised, and makes available for inspection the records necessary to demonstrate that it has been correctly assessed. The *Project Manager* reviews the records made available, and no later than thirteen weeks after the *Contractor's* notification

- accepts that part of Defined Cost as correct,

- notifies the *Contractor* that further records are needed or

- notifies the *Contractor* of errors in its assessment.

The *Contractor* provides any further records requested or advises the correction of the errors in its assessment within four weeks of the *Project Manager's* notification. The *Project Manager* reviews the records provided, and within four weeks

- accepts that part of Defined Cost as correct or

- notifies the *Contractor* of the correct assessment of that part of Defined Cost.

If the *Project Manager* does not notify a decision on that part of Defined Cost within the time stated, the *Contractor's* assessment is treated as correct.

Defined Cost	**52**	
	52.2	The *Contractor* keeps these records

- accounts of payments of Defined Cost,

- proof that the payments have been made,

- communications about and assessments of compensation events for Subcontractors and

- other records as stated in the Scope.

52.4 The *Contractor* allows the *Project Manager* to inspect at any time within working hours the accounts and records which it is required to keep.

CORE CLAUSES

MAIN OPTION CLAUSES

SECONDARY OPTION CLAUSES

COST COMPONENTS

CONTRACT DATA

OPTION F: MANAGEMENT CONTRACT

Identified and defined terms	**11** 11.2	(25) Defined Cost is

- the amount of payments due to Subcontractors for work which is subcontracted without taking account of amounts paid to or retained from the Subcontractor by the *Contractor* which would result in the *Client* paying or retaining the amount twice and

- the *prices* for work done by the *Contractor*

less Disallowed Cost.

(27) Disallowed Cost is cost which

- is not justified by the *Contractor's* accounts and records,

- should not have been paid to a Subcontractor or supplier in accordance with its contract,

- is a payment to a Subcontractor for

  – work which the Contract Data states that the *Contractor* will do itself or

  – the *Contractor's* management,

- was incurred only because the *Contractor* did not

  – follow an acceptance or procurement procedure stated in the Scope,

  – give an early warning which the contract required it to give or

  – give notification to the *Project Manager* of the preparation for and conduct of an adjudication or proceedings of a tribunal between the *Contractor* and a Subcontractor or supplier

and the cost of preparation for and conduct of an adjudication, or payments to a member of the Dispute Avoidance Board or proceedings of the *tribunal* between the Parties.

(31) The Price for Work Done to Date is the total Defined Cost which the *Project Manager* forecasts will have been paid by the *Contractor* before the next assessment date plus the Fee.

(34) The Prices are the forecast of the total Defined Cost for the whole of the *works* plus the Fee.

Providing the Works	**20** 20.2	The *Contractor* manages the *Contractor's* design, the provision of Site services and the construction and installation of the *works*. The *Contractor* subcontracts the *Contractor's* design, the provision of Site services and the construction and installation of the *works* except work which the Contract Data states that it will do.
	20.3	The *Contractor* advises the *Project Manager* on the practical implications of the design of the *works* and on subcontracting arrangements.
	20.4	The *Contractor* prepares forecasts of the total Defined Cost for the whole of the *works* in consultation with the *Project Manager* and submits them to the *Project Manager*. Forecasts are prepared at the intervals stated in the Contract Data from the *starting date* until Completion of the whole of the *works*. An explanation of the changes made since the previous forecast is submitted with each forecast.

Subcontracting	**26** 26.4	The *Contractor* submits the pricing information in the proposed subcontract documents for each subcontract to the *Project Manager* unless the *Project Manager* has agreed that no submission is required.

| Assessing the amount due | **50** | |
| | 50.8 | Payments of Defined Cost made by the *Contractor* in a currency other than the *currency of the contract* are included in the amount due as payments to be made to it in the same currency. Such payments are converted to the *currency of the contract* in order to calculate the Fee using the *exchange rates*. |

50.9 The *Contractor* notifies the *Project Manager* when the Defined Cost for a part of the *works* has been finalised, and makes available for inspection the records necessary to demonstrate that it has been correctly assessed. The *Project Manager* reviews the records made available, and no later than thirteen weeks after the *Contractor's* notification

- accepts that part of Defined Cost as correct,
- notifies the *Contractor* that further records are needed or
- notifies the *Contractor* of errors in its assessment.

The *Contractor* provides any further records requested or advises the correction of the errors in its assessment within four weeks of the *Project Manager's* notification. The *Project Manager* reviews the records provided, and within four weeks

- accepts that part of Defined Cost as correct or
- notifies the *Contractor* of the correct assessment of that part of Defined Cost.

If the *Project Manager* does not notify a decision on that part of Defined Cost within the time stated, the *Contractor's* assessment is treated as correct.

Defined Cost **52**

52.3 The *Contractor* keeps these records

- accounts of payments made to Subcontractors,
- proof that the payments have been made,
- communications about and assessments of compensation events for Subcontractors and
- other records as stated in the Scope.

52.4 The *Contractor* allows the *Project Manager* to inspect at any time within working hours the accounts and records which it is required to keep.

Assessing compensation events **63**

63.17 If work which the *Contractor* is to do is affected by a compensation event, the *Project Manager* and the *Contractor* agree the change to the price for the work and any change to the Completion Date and Key Dates. If they do not agree, the *Project Manager* decides the change.

CORE CLAUSES

MAIN OPTION CLAUSES

SECONDARY OPTION CLAUSES

COST COMPONENTS

CONTRACT DATA

Resolving and Avoiding Disputes

OPTION W1

Used when adjudication is the method of dispute resolution and the United Kingdom Housing Grants, Construction and Regeneration Act 1996 does not apply.

Resolving disputes   **W1**

W1.1   (1) A dispute arising under or in connection with the contract is referred to the *Senior Representatives* in accordance with the Dispute Reference Table. If the dispute is not resolved by the *Senior Representatives*, it is referred to and decided by the *Adjudicator*. A Party may replace a *Senior Representative* after notifying the other Party of the name of the replacement.

(2) The Party referring a dispute notifies the *Senior Representatives*, the other Party and the *Project Manager* of the nature of the dispute it wishes to resolve. Each Party submits to the other their statement of case within one week of the notification. Each statement of case is limited to no more than ten sides of A4 paper together with supporting evidence, unless otherwise agreed by the Parties.

(3) The *Senior Representatives* attend as many meetings and use any procedure they consider necessary to try to resolve the dispute over a period of no more than three weeks. At the end of this period the *Senior Representatives* produce a list of the issues agreed and issues not agreed. The *Project Manager* and the *Contractor* put into effect the issues agreed.

(4) No evidence of the statement of case or discussions is disclosed, used or referred to in any subsequent proceedings before the *Adjudicator* or the *tribunal*.

DISPUTE REFERENCE TABLE		
DISPUTE ABOUT	**WHICH PARTY MAY REFER IT TO THE *SENIOR REPRESENTATIVES*?**	**WHEN MAY IT BE REFERRED TO THE *SENIOR REPRESENTATIVES*?**
An action or inaction of the *Project Manager* or the *Supervisor*	Either Party	Not more than four weeks after the Party becomes aware of the action or inaction
A programme, compensation event or quotation for a compensation event which is treated as having been accepted	The *Client*	Not more than four weeks after it was treated as accepted
An assessment of Defined Cost which is treated as correct	Either Party	Not more than four weeks after the assessment was treated as correct
Any other matter	Either Party	When the dispute arises

The *Adjudicator*   **W1.2**   (1) The Parties appoint the *Adjudicator* under the NEC Dispute Resolution Service Contract current at the *starting date*.

(2) The *Adjudicator* acts impartially and decides the dispute as an independent adjudicator and not as an arbitrator.

(3) If the *Adjudicator* is not identified in the Contract Data or if the *Adjudicator* resigns or is unable to act, the Parties choose a new adjudicator jointly. If the Parties have not chosen an adjudicator, either Party may ask the *Adjudicator nominating body* to choose one. The *Adjudicator nominating body* chooses an adjudicator within seven days of the request. The chosen adjudicator becomes the *Adjudicator*.

(4) A replacement *Adjudicator* has the power to decide a dispute referred to a predecessor but not decided at the time when the predecessor resigned or became unable to act. The *Adjudicator* deals with an undecided dispute as if it had been referred on the date of appointment as replacement *Adjudicator.*

(5) The *Adjudicator* and the *Adjudicator's* employees and agents are not liable to the Parties for any action or failure to take action in an adjudication unless the action or failure to take action was in bad faith.

The adjudication W1.3

(1) A Party disputing any issue not agreed by the *Senior Representatives* issues a notice of adjudication to the other Party and the *Project Manager* within two weeks of the production of the list of agreed and not agreed issues, or when it should have been produced. The dispute is referred to the *Adjudicator* within one week of the notice of adjudication.

(2) The times for notifying and referring a dispute may be extended by the *Project Manager* if the *Contractor* and the *Project Manager* agree to the extension before the notice or referral is due. The *Project Manager* informs the *Contractor* of the extension that has been agreed. If a disputed matter is not notified and referred within the times set out in the contract, neither Party may subsequently refer it to the *Adjudicator* or the *tribunal.*

(3) The Party referring the dispute to the *Adjudicator* includes with its referral information to be considered by the *Adjudicator.* Any more information from a Party to be considered by the *Adjudicator* is provided within four weeks of the referral. This period may be extended if the *Adjudicator* and the Parties agree.

(4) If a matter disputed by the *Contractor* under or in connection with a subcontract is also a matter disputed under or in connection with the contract and if the subcontract allows, the *Contractor* may refer the subcontract dispute to the *Adjudicator* at the same time as the main contract referral. The *Adjudicator* then decides the disputes together and references to the Parties for the purposes of the dispute are interpreted as including the Subcontractor.

(5) The *Adjudicator* may

- review and revise any action or inaction of the *Project Manager* or *Supervisor* related to the dispute and alter a matter which has been treated as accepted or correct,

- take the initiative in ascertaining the facts and the law related to the dispute,

- instruct a Party to provide further information related to the dispute within a stated time and

- instruct a Party to take any other action which is considered necessary for the *Adjudicator* to reach a decision and to do so within a stated time.

(6) A communication between a Party and the *Adjudicator* is communicated to the other Party at the same time.

(7) If the *Adjudicator's* decision includes assessment of additional cost or delay caused to the *Contractor,* the assessment is made in the same way as a compensation event is assessed.

(8) The *Adjudicator* decides the dispute and informs the Parties and the *Project Manager* of the decision and reasons within four weeks of the end of the period for receiving information. This four week period may be extended if the Parties agree.

(9) Unless and until the *Adjudicator* has informed the Parties of the decision, the Parties, the *Project Manager* and the *Supervisor* proceed as if the matter disputed was not disputed.

(10) The *Adjudicator's* decision is binding on the Parties unless and until revised by the *tribunal* and is enforceable as a matter of contractual obligation between the Parties and not as an arbitral award. The *Adjudicator's* decision is final and binding if neither Party has notified the other within the times required by the contract that it is dissatisfied with a decision of the *Adjudicator* and intends to refer the matter to the *tribunal.* A Party does not refer a dispute to the *Adjudicator* that is the same or substantially the same as one that has already been referred to the *Adjudicator.*

(11) The *Adjudicator* may, within two weeks of giving the decision to the Parties, correct any clerical mistake or ambiguity.

The *tribunal*   W1.4   (1) A Party does not refer any dispute under or in connection with the contract to the *tribunal* unless it has first been referred to the *Adjudicator* in accordance with the contract.

(2) If, after being informed of the *Adjudicator's* decision, a Party is dissatisfied, that Party may notify the other Party of the matter which is disputed and state that it intends to refer the matter to the *tribunal*. The dispute is not referred to the *tribunal* unless this notification is given within four weeks of being informed of the *Adjudicator's* decision.

(3) If the *Adjudicator* does not inform the Parties of the decision within the time provided by the contract, a Party may notify the other Party that it intends to refer the dispute to the *tribunal*. A Party does not refer a dispute to the *tribunal* unless this notification is given within four weeks of the date by which the *Adjudicator* should have informed the Parties of the decision.

(4) The *tribunal* settles the dispute referred to it. The *tribunal* has the powers to reconsider any decision of the *Adjudicator* and review and revise any action or inaction of the *Project Manager* or the *Supervisor* related to the dispute. A Party is not limited in the *tribunal* proceedings to the information, evidence or arguments put to the *Adjudicator*.

(5) If the *tribunal* is arbitration, the *arbitration procedure*, the place where the arbitration is to be held and the method of choosing the arbitrator are those stated in the Contract Data.

(6) A Party does not call the *Adjudicator* as a witness in *tribunal* proceedings.

OPTION W2

Used when adjudication is the method of dispute resolution and the United Kingdom Housing Grants, Construction and Regeneration Act 1996 applies.

Resolving disputes	**W2** W2.1	(1) If the Parties agree, a dispute arising under or in connection with the contract is referred to the *Senior Representatives*. If the dispute is not resolved by the *Senior Representatives*, it is referred to and decided by the *Adjudicator*. A Party may replace a *Senior Representative* after notifying the other Party of the name of the replacement.

(2) The Party referring a dispute notifies the *Senior Representatives*, the other Party and the *Project Manager* of the nature of the dispute it wishes to resolve. Each Party submits to the other their statement of case within one week of the notification. Each statement of case is limited to no more than ten sides of A4 paper together with supporting evidence, unless otherwise agreed by the Parties.

(3) The *Senior Representatives* attend as many meetings and use any procedure they consider necessary to try to resolve the dispute over a period of up to three weeks. At the end of this period the *Senior Representatives* produce a list of the issues agreed and issues not agreed. The *Project Manager* and the *Contractor* put into effect the issues agreed.

(4) No evidence of the statement of case or discussions is disclosed, used or referred to in any subsequent proceedings before the *Adjudicator* or the *tribunal*.

The *Adjudicator*   W2.2   (1) A dispute arising under or in connection with the contract is referred to and decided by the *Adjudicator*. A Party may refer a dispute to the *Adjudicator* at any time whether or not the dispute has been referred to the *Senior Representatives*.

(2) In this Option, time periods stated in days exclude Christmas Day, Good Friday and bank holidays.

(3) The Parties appoint the *Adjudicator* under the NEC Dispute Resolution Service Contract current at the *starting date*.

(4) The *Adjudicator* acts impartially and decides the dispute as an independent adjudicator and not as an arbitrator.

(5) If the *Adjudicator* is not identified in the Contract Data or if the *Adjudicator* resigns or becomes unable to act

- the Parties may choose an adjudicator jointly or

- a Party may ask the *Adjudicator nominating body* to choose an adjudicator.

The *Adjudicator nominating body* chooses an adjudicator within four days of the request. The chosen adjudicator becomes the *Adjudicator*.

(6) A replacement *Adjudicator* has the power to decide a dispute referred to a predecessor but not decided at the time when the predecessor resigned or became unable to act. The *Adjudicator* deals with an undecided dispute as if it had been referred on the date of appointment as replacement *Adjudicator*.

(7) A Party does not refer a dispute to the *Adjudicator* that is the same or substantially the same as one that has already been decided by the *Adjudicator*.

(8) The *Adjudicator,* and the *Adjudicator's* employees and agents are not liable to the Parties for any action or failure to take action in an adjudication unless the action or failure to take action was in bad faith.

The adjudication   W2.3   (1) Before a Party refers a dispute to the *Adjudicator*, it gives a notice of adjudication to the other Party with a brief description of the dispute and the decision which it wishes the *Adjudicator* to make. If the *Adjudicator* is named in the Contract Data, the Party sends a copy of the notice of adjudication to the *Adjudicator* when it is issued. Within three days of the receipt of the notice of adjudication, the *Adjudicator* informs the Parties that the *Adjudicator*

CORE CLAUSES

MAIN OPTION CLAUSES

SECONDARY OPTION CLAUSES

COST COMPONENTS

CONTRACT DATA

- is able to decide the dispute in accordance with the contract or

- is unable to decide the dispute and has resigned.

If the *Adjudicator* does not so inform within three days of the issue of the notice of adjudication, either Party may act as if the *Adjudicator* has resigned.

(2) Within seven days of a Party giving a notice of adjudication it

- refers the dispute to the *Adjudicator*,

- provides the *Adjudicator* with the information on which it relies, including any supporting documents and

- provides a copy of the information and supporting documents it has provided to the *Adjudicator* to the other Party.

Any further information from a Party to be considered by the *Adjudicator* is provided within fourteen days of the referral. This period may be extended if the *Adjudicator* and the Parties agree.

(3) If a matter disputed by the *Contractor* under or in connection with a subcontract is also a matter disputed under or in connection with the contract, the *Contractor* may, with the consent of the Subcontractor, refer the subcontract dispute to the *Adjudicator* at the same time as the main contract referral. The *Adjudicator* then decides the disputes together and references to the Parties for the purposes of the dispute are interpreted as including the Subcontractor.

(4) The *Adjudicator* may

- review and revise any action or inaction of the *Project Manager* or *Supervisor* related to the dispute and alter a matter which has been treated as accepted or correct,

- take the initiative in ascertaining the facts and the law related to the dispute,

- instruct a Party to provide further information related to the dispute within a stated time and

- instruct a Party to take any other action which is considered necessary to reach a decision and to do so within a stated time.

(5) If a Party does not comply with any instruction within the time stated by the *Adjudicator*, the *Adjudicator* may continue the adjudication and make a decision based upon the information and evidence received.

(6) A communication between a Party and the *Adjudicator* is communicated to the other Party at the same time.

(7) If the *Adjudicator's* decision includes assessment of additional cost or delay caused to the *Contractor,* the assessment is made in the same way as a compensation event is assessed. If the *Adjudicator's* decision changes an amount notified as due, the date on which payment of the changed amount becomes due is seven days after the date of the decision.

(8) The *Adjudicator* decides the dispute and informs the Parties and the *Project Manager* of the decision and reasons within twenty eight days of the dispute being referred. This period may be extended by up to fourteen days with the consent of the referring Party or by any other period agreed by the Parties. The *Adjudicator* may in the decision allocate the *Adjudicator's* fees and expenses between the Parties.

(9) Unless and until the *Adjudicator* has informed the Parties of the decision, the Parties, the *Project Manager* and the *Supervisor* proceed as if the matter disputed was not disputed.

(10) If the *Adjudicator* does not inform the Parties of the decision within the time provided by the contract, the Parties and the *Adjudicator* may agree to extend the period for making a decision. If they do not agree to an extension, either Party may act as if the *Adjudicator* has resigned.

CORE CLAUSES

MAIN OPTION CLAUSES

SECONDARY OPTION CLAUSES

COST COMPONENTS

CONTRACT DATA

(11) The *Adjudicator's* decision is binding on the Parties unless and until revised by the *tribunal* and is enforceable as a matter of contractual obligation between the Parties and not as an arbitral award. The *Adjudicator's* decision is final and binding if neither Party has notified the other within the times required by the contract that it is dissatisfied with a matter decided by the *Adjudicator* and intends to refer the matter to the *tribunal*.

(12) The *Adjudicator* may, within five days of giving the decision to the Parties, correct the decision to remove a clerical or typographical error arising by accident or omission.

| The *tribunal* | W2.4 | (1) A Party does not refer any dispute under or in connection with the contract to the *tribunal* unless it has first been decided by the *Adjudicator* in accordance with the contract. |

(2) If, after the *Adjudicator* makes a decision, a Party is dissatisfied, that Party may notify the other Party of the matter which is disputed and state that it intends to refer the disputed matter to the *tribunal*. The dispute may not be referred to the *tribunal* unless this notification is given within four weeks of being informed of the *Adjudicator's* decision.

(3) The *tribunal* settles the dispute referred to it. The *tribunal* has the power to reconsider any decision of the *Adjudicator* and to review and revise any action or inaction of the *Project Manager* or the *Supervisor* related to the dispute. A Party is not limited in *tribunal* proceedings to the information, evidence or arguments put to the *Adjudicator*.

(4) If the *tribunal* is arbitration, the *arbitration procedure,* the place where the arbitration is to be held and the method of choosing the arbitrator are those stated in the Contract Data.

(5) A Party does not call the *Adjudicator* as a witness in *tribunal* proceedings.

CORE CLAUSES

MAIN OPTION CLAUSES

SECONDARY OPTION CLAUSES

COST COMPONENTS

CONTRACT DATA

OPTION W3

Used when a Dispute Avoidance Board is the method of dispute resolution and the United Kingdom Housing Grants, Construction and Regeneration Act 1996 does not apply.

The Dispute	W3	
Avoidance Board	W3.1	(1) The Dispute Avoidance Board consists of one or three members as identified in the Contract Data. If the Contract Data states that the number of members is three, the third member is jointly chosen by the Parties.

(2) The Parties appoint the Dispute Avoidance Board under the NEC Dispute Resolution Service Contract current at the *starting date*.

(3) The Dispute Avoidance Board acts impartially.

(4) If a member of the Dispute Avoidance Board is not identified in the Contract Data or if a member of the Dispute Avoidance Board is unable to act, the Parties jointly choose a new member. If the Parties have not chosen a Dispute Avoidance Board member or a replacement, either Party may ask the *Dispute Avoidance Board nominating body* to choose one. The *Dispute Avoidance Board nominating body* chooses a Dispute Avoidance Board member within seven days of the request. The chosen member becomes a member of the Dispute Avoidance Board.

(5) The Dispute Avoidance Board visits the Site at the intervals stated in the Contract Data from the *starting date* until the *defects date* unless the Parties agree that a visit is not necessary. The purpose of the visit is to enable the Dispute Avoidance Board to inspect the progress of the *works* and become aware of any potential disputes. The Dispute Avoidance Board makes additional visits when requested by the Parties.

(6) The agenda for the Site visit is proposed by the Parties and decided by the Dispute Avoidance Board.

(7) The members of the Dispute Avoidance Board, their employees and agents are not liable to the Parties for any action or failure to take action in resolving a potential dispute unless the action or failure to take action was in bad faith.

Resolving potential W3.2
disputes

(1) The Dispute Avoidance Board assists the Parties in resolving potential disputes before they become disputes.

(2) A potential dispute arising under or in connection with the contract is referred to the Dispute Avoidance Board.

(3) Potential disputes are notified and referred to the Dispute Avoidance Board between two to four weeks after notification of the issue to the other Party and the *Project Manager*.

(4) The Parties make available to the Dispute Avoidance Board

- copies of the contract,

- progress reports and

- any other material they consider relevant to any difference which they wish the Dispute Avoidance Board to consider in advance of the visit to the Site.

(5) The Dispute Avoidance Board

- visits the Site and inspects the *works*,

- reviews all potential disputes and helps the Parties to settle them without the need for the dispute to be formally referred,

- prepares a note of their visit and

- unless the Parties have resolved the potential dispute by the end of the Site visit, provide a recommendation for resolving it.

(6) The Dispute Avoidance Board can take the initiative in reviewing potential disputes, including asking the Parties to provide further information.

The *tribunal*   W3.3   (1) A Party does not refer any dispute under or in connection with the contract to the *tribunal* unless it has first been referred to the Dispute Avoidance Board as a potential dispute in accordance with the contract.

(2) If, after the Dispute Avoidance Board makes a recommendation, a Party is dissatisfied, that Party may notify the other Party of the matter which it disputes and state that it intends to refer it to the *tribunal*. The dispute is not referred to the *tribunal* unless this notification is given within four weeks of the provision of the Dispute Avoidance Board's recommendation.

(3) The *tribunal* settles the dispute referred to it. The *tribunal* has the powers to reconsider any recommendation of the Dispute Avoidance Board and review and revise any action or inaction of the *Project Manager* or the *Supervisor* related to the dispute. A Party is not limited in the *tribunal* proceedings to the information, evidence or arguments put to the Dispute Avoidance Board.

(4) If the *tribunal* is arbitration, the *arbitration procedure*, the place where the arbitration is to be held and the method of choosing the arbitrator are those stated in the Contract Data.

(5) A Party does not call a member of the Dispute Avoidance Board as a witness in *tribunal* proceedings.

Secondary Option Clauses

OPTION X1: PRICE ADJUSTMENT FOR INFLATION (USED ONLY WITH OPTIONS A, B, C AND D)

Defined terms	**X1**	
	X1.1	(a) The Base Date Index (B) is the latest available index before the *base date*.
		(b) The Latest Index (L) is the latest available index before the date of assessment of an amount due.
		(c) The Price Adjustment Factor (PAF) at each date of assessment of an amount due is the total of the products of each of the proportions stated in the Contract Data multiplied by $(L - B)/B$ for the index linked to it.
Price Adjustment Factor	X1.2	If an index is changed after it has been used in calculating a PAF, the calculation is not changed. The PAF calculated at the last assessment date before the Completion Date for the whole of the *works* is used for calculating an amount for price adjustment after that date.
Price adjustment Options A and B	X1.3	Each amount due includes an amount for price adjustment which is the sum of
		• the change in the Price for Work Done to Date since the last assessment of the amount due multiplied by the PAF and
		• the amount for price adjustment included in the previous amount due.
Price adjustment Options C and D	X1.4	Each time the amount due is assessed, an amount for price adjustment is added to the total of the Prices which is the change in the Price for Work Done to Date since the last assessment of the amount due multiplied by (PAF/(1+PAF)).
Compensation events	X1.5	The Defined Cost for compensation events is assessed using
		• the Defined Cost at *base date* levels for amounts calculated from rates stated in the Contract Data for people and Equipment and
		• the Defined Cost current at the dividing date used in assessing the compensation event, adjusted to the *base date* by dividing by one plus the PAF for the last assessment of the amount due before that dividing date, for other amounts.

OPTION X2: CHANGES IN THE LAW

Changes in the law	**X2**	
	X2.1	A change in the law of the country in which the Site is located is a compensation event if it occurs after the Contract Date. If the effect of a compensation event which is a change in the law is to reduce the total Defined Cost, the Prices are reduced.

OPTION X3: MULTIPLE CURRENCIES (USED ONLY WITH OPTIONS A AND B)

Multiple currencies	**X3**	
	X3.1	The *Contractor* is paid in currencies other than the *currency of the contract* for the items or activities listed in the Contract Data. The *exchange rates* are used to convert from the *currency of the contract* to other currencies.
	X3.2	Payments to the *Contractor* in currencies other than the *currency of the contract* do not exceed the maximum amounts stated in the Contract Data. Any excess is paid in the *currency of the contract*.

OPTION X4: ULTIMATE HOLDING COMPANY GUARANTEE

Ultimate holding company guarantee

X4

X4.1 If the *Contractor* is a subsidiary of another company, the *Contractor* gives to the *Client* a guarantee of the *Contractor's* performance from the ultimate holding company of the *Contractor* in the form set out in the Scope. If the guarantee was not given by the Contract Date, it is given to the *Client* within four weeks of the Contract Date.

X4.2 The *Contractor* may propose an alternative guarantor who is also owned by the ultimate holding company for acceptance by the *Project Manager*. A reason for not accepting the guarantor is that its commercial position is not strong enough to carry the guarantee.

OPTION X5: SECTIONAL COMPLETION

Sectional Completion

X5

X5.1 In these *conditions of contract*, unless stated as the whole of the *works*, each reference and clause relevant to

- the *works*,

- Completion and

- Completion Date

applies, as the case may be, to either the whole of the *works* or any *section* of the *works*.

OPTION X6: BONUS FOR EARLY COMPLETION

Bonus for early Completion

X6

X6.1 The *Contractor* is paid a bonus calculated at the rate stated in the Contract Data for each day from the earlier of

- Completion and

- the date on which the *Client* takes over the *works*

until the Completion Date.

OPTION X7: DELAY DAMAGES

Delay damages

X7

X7.1 The *Contractor* pays delay damages at the rate stated in the Contract Data for each day from the Completion Date until the earlier of

- Completion,

- the date on which the *Client* takes over the *works* and

- the date on which the *Project Manager* issues a termination certificate.

X7.2 If the Completion Date is changed to a later date after delay damages have been paid, the *Client* repays the overpayment of damages with interest. Interest is assessed from the date of payment to the date of repayment.

X7.3 If the *Client* takes over a part of the *works* before Completion, the delay damages are reduced from the date on which the part is taken over. The *Project Manager* assesses the benefit to the *Client* of taking over the part of the *works* as a proportion of the benefit to the *Client* of taking over the whole of the *works* not previously taken over. The delay damages are reduced in this proportion.

OPTION X8: UNDERTAKINGS TO THE *CLIENT* OR OTHERS

Undertakings to the *Client* or Others	**X8**	
	X8.1	The *Contractor* gives *undertakings to Others* as stated in the Contract Data.
	X8.2	If the *Contractor* subcontracts the work stated in the Contract Data it arranges for the Subcontractor to provide a *Subcontractor undertaking to Others* if required by the *Client*.
	X8.3	If the *Contractor* subcontracts the work stated in the Contract Data it arranges for the Subcontractor to provide a *Subcontractor undertaking to the Client*.
	X8.4	The *undertakings to Others*, *Subcontractor undertaking to Others* and *Subcontractor undertaking to the Client* are in the form set out in the Scope.
	X8.5	The *Client* prepares the undertakings and sends them to the *Contractor* for signature. The *Contractor* signs the undertakings, or arranges for the Subcontractor to sign them, and returns them to the *Client* within three weeks.

OPTION X9: TRANSFER OF RIGHTS

Transfer of rights	**X9**	
	X9.1	The *Client* owns the *Contractor's* rights over material prepared for the design of the *works* except as stated otherwise in the Scope. The *Contractor* obtains other rights for the *Client* as stated in the Scope and obtains from a Subcontractor equivalent rights for the *Client* over the material prepared by the Subcontractor. The *Contractor* provides to the *Client* the documents which transfer these rights to the *Client*.

OPTION X10: INFORMATION MODELLING

Defined terms	**X10**	
	X10.1	(1) The Information Execution Plan is the *information execution plan* or is the latest Information Execution Plan accepted by the *Project Manager*. The latest Information Execution Plan accepted by the *Project Manager* supersedes the previous Information Execution Plan.
		(2) Project Information is information provided by the *Contractor* which is used to create or change the Information Model.
		(3) The Information Model is the electronic integration of Project Information and similar information provided by the *Client* and other Information Providers and is in the form stated in the Information Model Requirements.
		(4) The Information Model Requirements are the requirements identified in the Scope for creating or changing the Information Model.
		(5) Information Providers are the people or organisations who contribute to the Information Model and are identified in the Information Model Requirements.
Collaboration	X10.2	The *Contractor* collaborates with other Information Providers as stated in the Information Model Requirements.
Early warning	X10.3	The *Contractor* and the *Project Manager* give an early warning by notifying the other as soon as either becomes aware of any matter which could adversely affect the creation or use of the Information Model.
Information Execution Plan	X10.4	(1) If an Information Execution Plan is not identified in the Contract Data, the *Contractor* submits a first Information Execution Plan to the *Project Manager* for acceptance within the period stated in the Contract Data.
		(2) Within two weeks of the *Contractor* submitting an Information Execution Plan for acceptance, the *Project Manager* notifies the *Contractor* of the acceptance of the Information Execution Plan or the reasons for not accepting it. A reason for not accepting an Information Execution Plan is that

- it does not comply with the Information Model Requirements or

- it does not allow the *Contractor* to Provide the Works.

If the *Project Manager* does not notify acceptance or non-acceptance within the time allowed, the *Contractor* may notify the *Project Manager* of that failure. If the failure continues for a further one week after the *Contractor's* notification, it is treated as acceptance by the *Project Manager* of the Information Execution Plan.

(3) The *Contractor* submits a revised Information Execution Plan to the *Project Manager* for acceptance

- within the *period for reply* after the *Project Manager* has instructed it to and

- when the *Contractor* chooses to.

(4) The *Contractor* provides the Project Information in the form stated in the Information Model Requirements and in accordance with the accepted Information Execution Plan.

Compensation events	X10.5	If the Information Execution Plan is altered by a compensation event, the *Contractor* includes the alterations to the Information Execution Plan in the quotation for the compensation event.
Use of the Information Model	X10.6	The *Client* owns the Information Model and the *Contractor's* rights over Project Information except as stated otherwise in the Information Model Requirements. The *Contractor* obtains from a Subcontractor equivalent rights for the *Client* over information prepared by the Subcontractor. The *Contractor* provides to the *Client* the documents which transfer these rights to the *Client*.
Liability	X10.7	(1) The following are *Client's* liabilities.

- A fault in the Information Model not caused by a Defect in the Project Information.

- A fault in information provided by Information Providers other than the *Contractor*.

(2) The *Contractor* is not liable for a Defect in the Project Information unless it failed to provide the Project Information using the skill and care normally used by professionals providing information similar to the Project Information.

(3) The *Contractor* provides insurance for claims made against it arising out of its failure to provide the Project Information using the skill and care normally used by professionals providing information similar to the Project Information. The minimum amount of this insurance is as stated in the Contract Data. This insurance provides cover from the *starting date* until the end of the period stated in the Contract Data.

OPTION X11: TERMINATION BY THE *CLIENT*

Termination by the *Client*	**X11**	
	X11.1	The *Client* may terminate the *Contractor's* obligation to Provide the Works for a reason not identified in the Termination Table by notifying the *Project Manager* and the *Contractor*.
	X11.2	If the *Client* terminates for a reason not identified in the Termination Table the termination procedures followed are P1 and P2 and the amounts due on termination are A1, A2 and A4.

OPTION X12: MULTIPARTY COLLABORATION (NOT USED WITH OPTION X20)

Identified and defined terms	**X12**	
	X12.1	(1) Partners are those who have a contract in connection with the subject matter of the contract which includes this multiparty collaboration Option or equivalent. The *Promoter* is a Partner.

CORE CLAUSES

MAIN OPTION CLAUSES

SECONDARY OPTION CLAUSES

COST COMPONENTS

CONTRACT DATA

(2) The Schedule of Partners is a list of the Partners which is in the document the Contract Data states it is in and Partners subsequently added by agreement of the Partners. It sets out the objectives of the Partners and includes targets for performance.

(3) An Own Contract is a contract between two Partners.

(4) The Core Group comprises the Partners selected to take decisions on behalf of the Partners.

(5) The Schedule of Core Group Members is a list of the Partners forming the Core Group.

(6) Partnering Information is information which specifies how the Partners collaborate and is either in the documents which the Contract Data states it is in or in an instruction given in accordance with the contract.

(7) A Key Performance Indicator is an aspect of performance for which a target is stated in the Schedule of Partners.

Actions	X12.2	(1) The Partners collaborate with each other to achieve the *Promoter's objective* stated in the Contract Data and the objectives of every other Partner stated in the Schedule of Partners.

(2) Each Partner nominates a representative to act for it in dealings with other Partners.

(3) The Core Group acts and takes decisions on behalf of the Partners on those matters stated in the Partnering Information.

(4) The Partners select the members of the Core Group. The Core Group decides how they will work and decides the dates when each member joins and leaves the Core Group. The *Promoter's* representative leads the Core Group unless stated otherwise in the Partnering Information.

(5) The Core Group keeps the Schedule of Core Group Members and the Schedule of Partners up to date and issues copies of them to the Partners each time either is revised.

(6) This Option does not create a legal partnership between Partners who are not one of the Parties in the contract.

Collaboration	X12.3	(1) The Partners collaborate as stated in the Partnering Information and in a spirit of mutual trust and co-operation.

(2) A Partner may ask another Partner to provide information which it needs to carry out the work in its Own Contract and the other Partner provides it.

(3) Each Partner gives an early warning to the other Partners when it becomes aware of any matter that could affect the achievement of another Partner's objectives stated in the Schedule of Partners.

(4) The Partners use common information systems as set out in the Partnering Information.

(5) A Partner implements a decision of the Core Group by issuing instructions in accordance with its Own Contracts.

(6) The Core Group may give an instruction to the Partners to change the Partnering Information. Each such change to the Partnering Information is a compensation event which may lead to reduced Prices.

(7) The Core Group prepares and maintains a timetable showing the proposed timing of the contributions of the Partners. The Core Group issues a copy of the timetable to the Partners each time it is revised. The *Contractor* changes its programme if it is necessary to do so in order to comply with the revised timetable. Each such change is a compensation event which may lead to reduced Prices.

(8) A Partner gives advice, information and opinion to the Core Group and to other Partners when asked to do so by the Core Group. This advice, information and opinion relates to work that another Partner is to carry out under its Own Contract and is given fully, openly and objectively. The Partners show contingency and risk allowances in information about costs, prices and timing for future work.

(9) A Partner informs the Core Group before subcontracting any work.

Incentives	X12.4	(1) A Partner is paid the amount stated in the Schedule of Partners if the target stated for a Key Performance Indicator is improved upon or achieved. Payment of the amount is due when the target has been improved upon or achieved and is made as part of the amount due in the Partner's Own Contract.

(2) The *Promoter* may add a Key Performance Indicator and associated payment to the Schedule of Partners but may not delete or reduce a payment stated in the Schedule of Partners.

OPTION X13: PERFORMANCE BOND

Performance bond	X13	
	X13.1	The *Contractor* gives the *Client* a performance bond, provided by a bank or insurer which the *Project Manager* has accepted, for the amount stated in the Contract Data and in the form set out in the Scope. A reason for not accepting the bank or insurer is that its commercial position is not strong enough to carry the bond. If the bond was not given by the Contract Date, it is given to the *Client* within four weeks of the Contract Date.

OPTION X14: ADVANCED PAYMENT TO THE *CONTRACTOR*

Advanced payment	X14	
	X14.1	The *Client* makes an advanced payment to the *Contractor* of the amount stated in the Contract Data. The advanced payment is included in the assessment made at the first assessment date or, if an advanced payment bond is required, at the next assessment date after the *Client* receives the advanced payment bond.
	X14.2	The advanced payment bond is issued by a bank or insurer which the *Project Manager* has accepted. A reason for not accepting the proposed bank or insurer is that its commercial position is not strong enough to carry the bond. The bond is for the amount of the advanced payment which the *Contractor* has not repaid and is in the form set out in the Scope. Delay in making the advanced payment in accordance with the contract is a compensation event.
	X14.3	The advanced payment is repaid to the *Client* by the *Contractor* in instalments of the amount stated in the Contract Data. An instalment is included in each amount due assessed after the period stated in the Contract Data has passed until the advanced payment has been repaid.

OPTION X15: THE *CONTRACTOR'S* DESIGN

The *Contractor's* design	X15	
	X15.1	The *Contractor* is not liable for a Defect which arose from its design unless it failed to carry out that design using the skill and care normally used by professionals designing works similar to the *works*.
	X15.2	If the *Contractor* corrects a Defect for which it is not liable under the contract it is a compensation event.
	X15.3	The *Contractor* may use the material provided by it under the contract for other work unless

- the ownership of the material has been given to the *Client* or

- it is stated otherwise in the Scope.

X15.4 The *Contractor* retains copies of drawings, specifications, reports and other documents which record the *Contractor's* design for the *period for retention*. The copies are retained in the form stated in the Scope.

X15.5 The *Contractor* provides insurance for claims made against it arising out of its failure to use the skill and care normally used by professionals designing works similar to the *works*. The minimum amount of this insurance is as stated in the Contract Data. This insurance provides cover from the *starting date* until the end of the period stated in the Contract Data.

X15.6 Before the *starting date* and on each renewal of the insurance policy until the *defects date*, the *Contractor* submits to the *Project Manager* for acceptance a certificate which states that the insurance required by this clause is in force.

After the *defects date* and on each renewal of the insurance policy until the end of the period stated in the Contract Data for which insurance is to be maintained, the *Contractor* submits to the *Client* for acceptance a certificate which states that the insurance required by this clause is in force. The certificate is signed by the *Contractor's* insurer or insurance broker.

The *Project Manager* or the *Client* accepts the certificate if the insurance complies with this clause and if the insurer's commercial position is strong enough to carry the insured liability. The *Client's* acceptance of an insurance certificate provided by the *Contractor* does not change the responsibility of the *Contractor* to provide the insurance stated in this clause.

OPTION X16: RETENTION (NOT USED WITH OPTION F)

Retention X16

X16.1 After the Price for Work Done to Date has reached the *retention free amount*, an amount is retained in each amount due. Until the earlier of

- Completion of the whole of the *works* and

- the date on which the *Client* takes over the whole of the *works*

the amount retained is the *retention percentage* applied to the excess of the Price for Work Done to Date above the *retention free amount*.

X16.2 The amount retained is halved

- in the next assessment made after Completion of the whole of the *works* or

- in the next assessment after the *Client* has taken over the whole of the *works* if this is before Completion of the whole of the *works*.

The amount retained remains at this amount until the date when the Defects Certificate is due to be issued. No amount is retained in the assessments made after the Defects Certificate is due to be issued.

X16.3 If stated in the Contract Data or agreed by the *Client*, the *Contractor* may give the *Client* a retention bond, provided by a bank or insurer which the *Project Manager* has accepted, for the total amount to be retained and in the form set out in the Scope. A reason for not accepting the bank or insurer is that its commercial position is not strong enough to carry the bond. Any amount retained after the *Contractor* gives the *Client* a retention bond is paid to the *Contractor* in the next assessment.

OPTION X17: LOW PERFORMANCE DAMAGES

Low performance damages X17

X17.1 If a Defect included in the Defects Certificate shows low performance with respect to a performance level stated in the Contract Data, the *Contractor* pays the amount of low performance damages stated in the Contract Data.

OPTION X18: LIMITATION OF LIABILITY

Limitation of liability

X18

X18.1 Each of the limits to the *Contractor's* liability in this clause apply if a limit is stated in the Contract Data.

X18.2 The *Contractor's* liability to the *Client* for the *Client's* indirect or consequential loss is limited to the amount stated in the Contract Data.

X18.3 For any one event, the liability of the *Contractor* to the *Client* for loss of or damage to the *Client's* property is limited to the amount stated in the Contract Data.

X18.4 The *Contractor's* liability to the *Client* for Defects due to its design which are not listed on the Defects Certificate is limited to the amount stated in the Contract Data.

X18.5 The *Contractor's* total liability to the *Client* for all matters arising under or in connection with the contract, other than the excluded matters, is limited to the amount stated in the Contract Data and applies in contract, tort or delict and otherwise to the extent allowed under the *law of the contract*.

The excluded matters are amounts payable by the *Contractor* as stated in the contract for

- loss of or damage to the *Client's* property,

- delay damages if Option X7 applies,

- low performance damages if Option X17 applies and

- *Contractor's* share if Option C or Option D applies.

X18.6 The *Contractor* is not liable to the *Client* for a matter unless details of the matter are notified to the *Contractor* before the *end of liability date*.

OPTION X20: KEY PERFORMANCE INDICATORS (NOT USED WITH OPTION X12)

Incentives

X20

X20.1 A Key Performance Indicator is an aspect of performance by the *Contractor* for which a target is stated in the Incentive Schedule. The Incentive Schedule is the *incentive schedule* unless later changed in accordance with the contract.

X20.2 From the *starting date* until the Defects Certificate has been issued, the *Contractor* reports to the *Project Manager* its performance against each of the Key Performance Indicators. Reports are provided at the intervals stated in the Contract Data and include the forecast final measurement against each indicator.

X20.3 If the *Contractor's* forecast final measurement against a Key Performance Indicator will not achieve the target stated in the Incentive Schedule, it submits to the *Project Manager* its proposals for improving performance.

X20.4 The *Contractor* is paid the amount stated in the Incentive Schedule if the target stated for a Key Performance Indicator is improved upon or achieved. Payment of the amount is due when the target has been improved upon or achieved.

X20.5 The *Client* may add a Key Performance Indicator and associated payment to the Incentive Schedule but may not delete or reduce a payment stated in the Incentive Schedule.

OPTION X21: WHOLE LIFE COST

Whole life cost

X21

X21.1 The *Contractor* may propose to the *Project Manager* that the Scope is changed in order to reduce the cost of operating and maintaining an asset.

X21.2 If the *Project Manager* is prepared to consider the change, the *Contractor* submits a quotation which comprises

- a detailed description,

- the forecast cost reduction to the *Client* of the asset over its whole life,

- an analysis of the resulting risks to the *Client*,

- the proposed changes to the Prices and

- a revised programme showing any changes to the Completion Date and Key Dates.

X21.3 The *Project Manager* consults with the *Contractor* about a quotation. The *Project Manager* replies within the *period for reply*. The reply is acceptance of the quotation or the reasons for not accepting it. The *Project Manager* may give any reason for not accepting the quotation.

X21.4 The *Project Manager* does not change the Scope as proposed by the *Contractor* unless the *Contractor's* quotation is accepted.

X21.5 When a quotation to reduce the costs of operating and maintaining an asset is accepted the *Project Manager* changes the Scope, the Prices, the Completion Date and the Key Dates accordingly and accepts the revised programme. The change to the Scope is not a compensation event.

OPTION X22: EARLY *CONTRACTOR* INVOLVEMENT (USED ONLY WITH OPTIONS C AND E)

Defined terms   **X22**

X22.1 (1) The Access Dates are the *access dates* unless later changed in accordance with the contract.

(2) Budget is the items and amounts stated in the Contract Data unless the amounts are later changed in accordance with the contract.

(3) Project Cost is the total paid by the *Client* to the *Contractor* and Others for the items included in the Budget.

(4) Stage One and Stage Two have the meanings given to them in the Scope.

(5) Pricing Information is information which specifies how the *Contractor* prepares its assessment of the Prices for Stage Two, and is in the document which the Contract Data states it is in.

Forecasts   X22.2 (1) The *Contractor* provides detailed forecasts of the total Defined Cost of the work to be done in Stage One for acceptance by the *Project Manager*. Forecasts are prepared at the intervals stated in the Contract Data from the *starting date* until the issue of a notice to proceed to Stage Two.

(2) Within one week of the *Contractor* submitting a forecast for acceptance, the *Project Manager* either accepts the forecast or notifies the *Contractor* of the reasons for not accepting it. A reason for not accepting the forecast is that

- it does not comply with the Scope or

- it includes work which is not necessary for Stage One.

(3) The *Contractor* makes a revised submission taking account of the *Project Manager's* reasons.

(4) The cost of any work that is not included in the accepted forecast is treated as a Disallowed Cost.

(5) The *Contractor* prepares forecasts of the Project Cost in consultation with the *Project Manager* and submits them to the *Project Manager*. Forecasts are prepared at the intervals stated in the Contract Data from the *starting date* until Completion of the whole of the *works*. An explanation of the changes made since the previous forecast is submitted with each forecast.

Proposals for Stage Two X22.3

(1) The *Contractor* prepares its proposals for Stage Two in consultation with the *Project Manager* and submits them to the *Project Manager* in accordance with the submission procedure stated in the Scope. The submission includes the *Contractor's* forecast of the effect of the proposals on the Project Cost and the Accepted Programme.

(2) At the end of Stage One the *Contractor* submits to the *Project Manager* for acceptance

- its proposals for Stage Two,

- a revised programme,

- any revisions to the Access Dates, Key Dates and the Completion Date and

- the total of the Prices or any change to the total of the Prices

in accordance with the submission procedure stated in the Scope.

If the main Option is C, the total of the Prices is in the form of revisions to the Activity Schedule. A revised Activity Schedule includes the Price for Work Done to Date in Stage One.

(3) If the submission is not accepted, the *Project Manager* gives reasons. A reason for not accepting a *Contractor's* submission is that

- it does not comply with the Scope,

- it will cause unnecessary delay to the Access Dates, Key Dates or the Completion Date,

- it will cause the *Client* to incur unnecessary costs to Others or

- the *Project Manager* is not satisfied that the total of the Prices or any changes to the total of the Prices have been properly assessed.

(4) The *Contractor* makes a revised submission taking account of the *Project Manager's* reasons.

(5) The total of the Prices for Stage Two is assessed by the *Contractor* using the Pricing Information stated in the Contract Data.

(6) The *Contractor* obtains approvals and consents from Others as stated in the Scope.

(7) Any additional Scope provided by the *Contractor* in Stage One becomes Scope provided by the *Contractor* for its design.

(8) The *Contractor* completes any outstanding design during Stage Two.

Key persons X22.4

The *Contractor* does not replace any *key person* during Stage One unless

- the *Project Manager* instructs the *Contractor* to do so or

- the person is unable to continue to act in connection with the contract.

Notice to proceed to Stage Two	X22.5	(1) The *Project Manager* issues a notice to proceed to Stage Two when

- the *Contractor* has obtained approvals and consents from Others as stated in the Scope,

- changes to the Budget have been agreed or assessed by the *Project Manager*,

- the *Project Manager* and the *Contractor* have agreed the total of the Prices for Stage Two, any changes to the Access Date, Key Dates and the Completion Date and

- the *Client* has confirmed the *works* are to proceed.

(2) If a notice to proceed to Stage Two is issued, the *Project Manager* changes the Prices, the Access Dates, the Key Dates and the Completion Date accordingly and accepts the revised programme.

(3) If a notice to proceed to Stage Two is not issued for any reason, the *Project Manager* issues an instruction that the work required in Stage Two is removed from the Scope. This instruction is not a compensation event.

(4) If the *Project Manager* does not issue a notice to proceed to Stage Two because

- the *Project Manager* and the *Contractor* have not agreed the total of the Prices or any changes to the Access Dates, Key Dates or the Completion Date,

- the *Contractor* has failed to achieve the performance requirements stated in the Scope

the *Client* may appoint another contractor to complete the Stage Two *works*.

Changes to the Budget	X22.6	(1) If one of the following events happens, the *Project Manager* and the *Contractor* discuss different ways of dealing with changes to the Budget which are practicable.

- The *Project Manager* gives an instruction changing the *Client's* requirements stated in the Scope.

- Additional events stated in the Contract Data.

(2) The *Project Manager* and the *Contractor* agree changes to the Budget within four weeks of the event arising which changes the Budget. If the *Project Manager* and the *Contractor* cannot agree the changes to the Budget the *Project Manager* assesses the change and notifies the *Contractor* of the assessment.

Incentive payment	X22.7	(1) If the final Project Cost is less than the Budget, the *Contractor* is paid the budget incentive. The budget incentive is calculated by multiplying the difference between the Budget and the final Project Cost by the percentage stated in the Contract Data.

(2) The *Project Manager* makes a preliminary assessment of the budget incentive at Completion of the whole of the *works* and includes this in the amount due following Completion of the whole of the *works*.

(3) The *Project Manager* makes a final assessment of the budget incentive and includes this in the final amount due.

Option Y

OPTION Y(UK)1: PROJECT BANK ACCOUNT

Project Bank Account	Y(UK)1	

Defined terms	Y1.1	(1) Joining Deed is an agreement in the form set out in the contract under which the Supplier joins the Trust Deed.

(2) Named Suppliers are *named suppliers* and other Suppliers who have signed the Joining Deed.

(3) The Payment Schedule is a list of payments to be made to the *Contractor* and Named Suppliers from the Project Bank Account.

(4) Project Bank Account is the account used to receive payments from the *Client* and the *Contractor* and to make payments to the *Contractor* and Named Suppliers.

(5) Project Bank Account Tracker is a register of all payments made to and from the Project Bank Account and the date each payment was made and is in the form stated in the Scope.

(6) A Supplier is a person or organisation who has a contract to

- construct or install part of the *works*,

- provide a service necessary to Provide the Works or

- supply Plant and Materials for the *works*.

(7) Trust Deed is an agreement in the form set out in the contract which contains provisions for administering the Project Bank Account.

Project Bank Account	Y1.2	The *account holder* establishes the Project Bank Account with the *project bank* within eight weeks of the Contract Date.
	Y1.3	Unless stated otherwise in the Contract Data, the *Contractor* pays any charges made and is paid any interest paid by the *project bank*. The charges and interest by the *project bank* are not included in Defined Cost.
	Y1.4	If the *account holder* is the *Contractor*, it submits to the *Project Manager* for acceptance details of the banking arrangements for the Project Bank Account. A reason for not accepting the banking arrangements is that they do not provide for payments and inspections to be made in accordance with the contract. The *Contractor* provides to the *Project Manager* copies of communications with the *project bank* in connection with the Project Bank Account.

Named Suppliers	Y1.5	The *Contractor* includes in its contracts with Named Suppliers the arrangements in the contract for the operation of the Project Bank Account and Trust Deed. The *Contractor* informs the Named Suppliers it appoints, the details of the Project Bank Account and the arrangements for payment of amounts due under their contracts.
	Y1.6	The *Contractor* submits proposals for adding a Supplier to the Named Suppliers to the *Project Manager* for acceptance. A submission includes the Suppliers stated in the Scope and other Suppliers requested by the *Contractor*. A reason for not accepting a submission is that the addition of a Supplier does not comply with the Scope. The *Client*, the *Contractor* and the Supplier sign the Joining Deed after acceptance.

Payments	Y1.7	Until the Project Bank Account is established, payment is made by the *Client* to the *Contractor*.
	Y1.8	The *Contractor* shows in the application for payment the amounts due to Named Suppliers in accordance with their contracts.

Y1.9   Within the time set out in the banking arrangements to allow the *project bank* to make payment to the *Contractor* and Named Suppliers in accordance with the contract,

● the *Contractor* prepares the Payment Schedule, provides a copy to the *Project Manager* and provides the information in the Payment Schedule to the *project bank,*

● the *Client* makes payment to the Project Bank Account of the amount which is due to be paid under the contract and

● the *Contractor* makes payment to the Project Bank Account of any amount which the *Client* has informed the *Contractor* it intends to withhold from the certified amount and which is required to make payment to Named Suppliers.

Y1.10   The *Contractor* notifies the *Project Manager* if the amount due to any Named Supplier stated in the Payment Schedule is different from that in the payment certificate and provides reasons for the change.

Y1.11   If the *account holder* is the *Contractor,* it authorises payment in accordance with the Payment Schedule no later than one day before the final date for payment. Following payment, the *Client* checks the amounts paid to the Named Suppliers by inspecting the Project Bank Account.

Y1.12   If the *account holder* is the Parties, they jointly authorise payment in accordance with the Payment Schedule no later than one day before the final date for payment.

Y1.13   Following authorisation, the *Contractor* and Named Suppliers receive payment from the Project Bank Account of the sums set out in the Payment Schedule as soon as practicable after the Project Bank Account receives payment.

Y1.14   The *Contractor* updates the Project Bank Account Tracker and submits it to the *Project Manager* within one week of any payment being made from the Project Bank Account.

Y1.15   A payment which is due from the *Contractor* to the *Client* is not made through the Project Bank Account.

Effect of Payment   Y1.16   Payments made from the Project Bank Account are treated as payments from the *Client* to the *Contractor* in accordance with the contract. A delay in payment due to a failure of the *Contractor* to comply with the requirements of this clause is not treated as late payment under the contract.

Trust Deed   Y1.17   The *Client,* the *Contractor* and *named suppliers* sign the Trust Deed within two weeks of the Contract Date.

Termination   Y1.18   If the *Project Manager* issues a termination certificate, no further payment is made into the Project Bank Account.

TRUST DEED

This agreement is made between the *Client*, the *Contractor* and the Named Suppliers.

Terms in this deed have the meanings given to them in the contract between . . . . and . . . . for . . . . (the *works*).

Background

The *Client* and the *Contractor* have entered into a contract for the *works*.

The Named Suppliers have entered into contracts with the *Contractor* or a Subcontractor in connection with the *works*.

A Project Bank Account will be established to make provision for payment to the *Contractor* and the Named Suppliers.

Agreement

The parties to this deed agree that

- sums due to the *Contractor* and Named Suppliers and set out in the Payment Schedule are held in trust in the Project Bank Account for distribution to the *Contractor* and Named Suppliers in accordance with the banking arrangements applicable to the Project Bank Account,

- further Named Suppliers may be added as parties to this deed with the agreement of the *Client* and *Contractor*. The agreement of the *Client* and *Contractor* is treated as agreement by the Named Suppliers who are parties to this deed,

- this deed is subject to the law of the contract for the *works*,

- the benefits under this deed may not be assigned.

Executed as a deed on . . . .

by

. . . . (*Client*)

. . . . (*Contractor*)

. . . .

. . . .

. . . . (Named Suppliers)

. . . .

CORE CLAUSES

MAIN OPTION CLAUSES

SECONDARY OPTION CLAUSES

COST COMPONENTS

CONTRACT DATA

JOINING DEED

This agreement is made between the *Client*, the *Contractor* and . . . . (the Additional Supplier).

Terms in this deed have the meanings given to them in the contract between . . . . and . . . . for . . . . (the *works*).

Background

The *Client* and the *Contractor* have entered into a contract for the *works*.

The Named Suppliers have entered into contracts with the *Contractor* or a Subcontractor in connection with the *works*.

A Project Bank Account **has been/will be** (delete as applicable) established to make provision for payment to the *Contractor* and the Named Suppliers.

The *Client,* the *Contractor* and the Named Suppliers have entered into a deed as set out in Annex 1 (the Trust Deed) and have agreed that the Additional Supplier may join that deed.

Agreement

The parties to this deed agree that

* the Additional Supplier becomes a party to the Trust Deed from the date set out below,

* this deed is subject to the law of the contract for the *works*,

* the benefits under this deed may not be assigned.

Executed as a deed on . . . .

by

. . . . (*Client*)

. . . . (*Contractor*)

. . . . (Additional Supplier)

OPTION Y(UK)2: THE HOUSING GRANTS, CONSTRUCTION AND REGENERATION ACT 1996

The Housing Grants, Construction and Regeneration Act 1996	Y(UK)2	
Definitions	Y2.1	In this Option, time periods stated in days exclude Christmas Day, Good Friday and bank holidays.
Dates for payment	Y2.2	The date on which a payment becomes due is seven days after the assessment date. The date on which the final payment becomes due is

    • if the *Project Manager* makes an assessment after the issue of a Defects Certificate, five weeks after the issue of the Defects Certificate,

    • if the *Project Manager* does not make an assessment after the issue of a Defects Certificate, one week after the *Contractor* issues its assessment or

    • if the *Project Manager* has issued a termination certificate, fourteen weeks after the issue of the certificate.

The final date for payment is fourteen days after the date on which payment becomes due or a different period for payment if stated in the Contract Data.

The *Project Manager's* certificate is the notice of payment specifying the amount due at the payment due date (the notified sum, which may be zero) and stating the basis on which the amount was calculated. If the *Project Manager* does not make an assessment after the issue of a Defects Certificate, the *Contractor's* assessment is the notice of payment.

Notice of intention to pay less	Y2.3	If either Party intends to pay less than the notified sum, it notifies the other Party not later than seven days (the prescribed period) before the final date for payment by stating the amount considered to be due and the basis on which that sum is calculated. A Party does not withhold payment of an amount due under the contract unless it has notified its intention to pay less than the notified sum as required by the contract.
	Y2.4	If the *Client* terminates for one of reasons R1 to R15, R18 or R22 and a certified payment has not been made at the date of the termination certificate, the *Client* makes the certified payment unless

    • it has notified the *Contractor* in accordance with the contract that it intends to pay less than the notified sum or

    • the termination is for one of reasons R1 to R10 and the reason occurred after the last date on which it could have notified the *Contractor* in accordance with the contract that it intends to pay less than the notified sum.

Suspension of performance	Y2.5	If the *Contractor* exercises its right under the Housing Grants, Construction and Regeneration Act 1996 as amended by the Local Democracy, Economic Development and Construction Act 2009 to suspend performance, it is a compensation event.

OPTION Y(UK)3: THE CONTRACTS (RIGHTS OF THIRD PARTIES) ACT 1999

Third party rights	Y(UK)3	
	Y3.1	A *beneficiary* may enforce the terms of the contract stated in the Contract Data under the Contracts (Rights of Third Parties) Act 1999.
	Y3.2	Other than the Parties or a *beneficiary*, no person can enforce any of the terms of the contract under the Contracts (Rights of Third Parties) Act 1999.
	Y3.3	If a *beneficiary* is identified by class or description and not as a named person or organisation, the *Client* notifies the *Contractor* of the name of the *beneficiary* once it has been identified.

CORE CLAUSES

MAIN OPTION CLAUSES

SECONDARY OPTION CLAUSES

COST COMPONENTS

CONTRACT DATA

OPTION Z: *ADDITIONAL CONDITIONS OF CONTRACT*

Additional conditions of contract

Z1

Z1.1 The *additional conditions of contract* stated in the Contract Data are part of the contract.

Schedule of Cost Components

This schedule is part of these *conditions of contract* only when Option C, D or E is used. An amount is included

- only in one cost component and

- only if it is incurred in order to Provide the Works.

People 1 The following components of

- the cost of people who are directly employed by the *Contractor* and whose normal place of working is within the Working Areas and

- the cost of people who are directly employed by the *Contractor* and whose normal place of working is not within the Working Areas but who are working in the Working Areas, proportionate to the time they spend working in the Working Areas.

11 Wages, salaries and amounts paid by the *Contractor* for people paid according to the time worked on the contract.

12 Payments related to work on the contract and made to people for

(a) bonuses and incentives

(b) overtime

(c) working in special circumstances

(d) special allowances

(e) absence due to sickness and holidays

(f) severance.

13 Payments made in relation to people in accordance with their employment contract for

(a) travel

(b) subsistence and lodging

(c) relocation

(d) medical examinations

(e) passports and visas

(f) travel insurance

(g) items (a) to (f) for dependants

(h) protective clothing

(i) contributions, levies or taxes imposed by law

(j) pensions and life assurance

(k) death benefit

(l) occupational accident benefits

(m) medical aid and health insurance

(n) a vehicle

(o) safety training.

14 The following components of the cost of people who are not directly employed by the *Contractor* but are paid for by the *Contractor* according to the time worked while they are within the Working Areas.

Amounts paid by the *Contractor*.

Equipment

2 The following components of the cost of Equipment which is used within the Working Areas.

21 Payments for the hire or rent of Equipment not owned by

- the *Contractor*,

- the *Contractor's* ultimate holding company or

- a company with the same ultimate holding company

at the hire or rental rate multiplied by the time for which the Equipment is required.

22 Payments for Equipment which is not listed in the Contract Data but is

- owned by the *Contractor*,

- purchased by the *Contractor* under a hire purchase or lease agreement or

- hired by the *Contractor* from the *Contractor's* ultimate holding company or from a company with the same ultimate holding company

at open market rates, multiplied by the time for which the Equipment is required.

23 Payments for Equipment purchased for work included in the contract listed with a time-related on cost charge, in the Contract Data, of

- the change in value over the period for which the Equipment is required and

- the time-related on cost charge stated in the Contract Data for the period for which the Equipment is required.

The change in value is the difference between the purchase price and either the sale price or the open market sale price at the end of the period for which the Equipment is required. Interim payments of the change in value are made at each assessment date. A final payment is made in the next assessment after the change in value has been determined.

If the *Project Manager* agrees, an additional item of Equipment may be assessed as if it had been listed in the Contract Data.

24 Payments for special Equipment listed in the Contract Data. These amounts are the rates stated in the Contract Data multiplied by the time for which the Equipment is required.

If the *Project Manager* agrees, an additional item of special Equipment may be assessed as if it had been listed in the Contract Data.

25 Payments for the purchase price of Equipment which is consumed.

26 Unless included in the hire or rental rates, payments for

- transporting Equipment to and from the Working Areas other than for repair and maintenance,

- erecting and dismantling Equipment and

- constructing, fabricating or modifying Equipment as a result of a compensation event.

27 Payments for purchase of materials used to construct or fabricate Equipment.

28 Unless included in the hire rates, the cost of operatives is included in the cost of people.

| **Plant and Materials** | 3 | The following components of the cost of Plant and Materials. |
| | 31 | Payments for |

- purchasing Plant and Materials,

- delivery to and removal from the Working Areas,

- providing and removing packaging and

- samples and tests.

| | 32 | Cost is credited with payments received for disposal of Plant and Materials unless the cost is disallowed. |

| **Subcontractors** | 4 | The following components of the cost of Subcontractors. |
| | 41 | Payments to Subcontractors for work which is subcontracted without taking into account any amounts paid to or retained from the Subcontractor by the *Contractor*, which would result in the *Client* paying or retaining the amount twice. |

| **Charges** | 5 | The following components of the cost of charges paid or received by the *Contractor*. |
| | 51 | Payments for the provision and use in the Working Areas of |

- water,

- gas,

- electricity,

- telephone and

- internet.

| | 52 | Payments to public authorities and other properly constituted authorities of charges which they are authorised to make in respect of the *works*. |
| | 53 | Payments for |

(a) cancellation charges arising from a compensation event

(b) buying or leasing land or buildings within the Working Areas

(c) compensation for loss of crops or buildings

(d) royalties

(e) inspection certificates

(f) charges for access to the Working Areas

(g) facilities for visits to the Working Areas by Others

(h) consumables and equipment provided by the *Contractor* for the *Project Manager's* and *Supervisor's* offices.

| | 54 | Payments made and received by the *Contractor* for the removal from Site and disposal or sale of materials from excavation and demolition. |

| **Manufacture and fabrication** | 6 | The following components of the cost of manufacture and fabrication of Plant and Materials by the *Contractor* which are |

- wholly or partly designed specifically for the *works* and

- manufactured or fabricated outside the Working Areas.

| | 61 | Amounts calculated by multiplying each of the rates for people in the Contract Data by the total time appropriate to that rate spent on manufacture and fabrication of Plant and Materials outside the Working Areas. |

Design	7	The following components of the cost of design of the *works* and Equipment done outside the Working Areas.
	71	Amounts calculated by multiplying each of the rates for people in the Contract Data by the total time appropriate to that rate spent on design of the *works* and Equipment outside the Working Areas.
	72	The cost of travel to and from the Working Areas for the categories of design people listed in the Contract Data.
Insurance	8	The following are deducted from cost

- the cost of events for which the contract requires the *Contractor* to insure and

- other costs paid to the *Contractor* by insurers.

Short Schedule of Cost Components

This schedule is part of these *conditions of contract* only when Option A or B is used. An amount is included

- only in one cost component and

- only if it is incurred in order to Provide the Works.

People

1 The following components of the cost of

- people who are directly employed by the *Contractor* and whose normal place of working is within the Working Areas,

- people who are directly employed by the *Contractor* and whose normal place of working is not within the Working Areas but who are working in the Working Areas, proportionate to the time they spend working in the Working Areas and

- people who are not directly employed by the *Contractor* but are paid for by it according to the time worked while they are within the Working Areas.

11 Amounts calculated by multiplying each of the People Rates by the total time appropriate to that rate spent within the Working Areas.

Equipment

2 The following components of the cost of Equipment which is used within the Working Areas.

21 Amounts for Equipment which is in the published list stated in the Contract Data. These amounts are calculated by applying the percentage adjustment for listed Equipment stated in the Contract Data to the rates in the published list and by multiplying the resulting rate by the time for which the Equipment is required.

22 Amounts for Equipment listed in the Contract Data which is not in the published list stated in the Contract Data. These amounts are the rates stated in the Contract Data multiplied by the time for which the Equipment is required.

23 The time required is expressed in hours, days, weeks or months consistent with the list of items of Equipment in the Contract Data or with the published list stated in the Contract Data.

24 Unless the item is in the published list and the rate includes the cost component, payments for

- transporting Equipment to and from the Working Areas other than for repair and maintenance,

- erecting and dismantling Equipment and

- constructing, fabricating or modifying Equipment as a result of a compensation event.

25 Unless the item is in the published list and the rate includes the cost component, the purchase price of Equipment which is consumed.

26 Unless included in the rate in the published list, the cost of operatives is included in the cost of people.

27 Amounts for Equipment which is neither in the published list stated in the Contract Data nor listed in the Contract Data, at competitively tendered or open market rates, multiplied by the time for which the Equipment is required.

CORE CLAUSES

MAIN OPTION CLAUSES

SECONDARY OPTION CLAUSES

COST COMPONENTS

CONTRACT DATA

CORE CLAUSES

MAIN OPTION CLAUSES

SECONDARY OPTION CLAUSES

COST COMPONENTS

CONTRACT DATA

Plant and Materials	3	The following components of the cost of Plant and Materials.
	31	Payments for

- purchasing Plant and Materials,
- delivery to and removal from the Working Areas,
- providing and removing packaging and
- samples and tests.

	32	Cost is credited with payments received for disposal of Plant and Materials unless the cost is disallowed.
Subcontractors	4	The following components of the cost of Subcontractors.
	41	Payments to Subcontractors for work which is subcontracted.
Charges	5	The following components of the cost of charges paid or received by the *Contractor*.
	51	Payments for the provision and use in the Working Areas of

- water,
- gas,
- electricity,
- telephone and
- internet.

	52	Payments to public authorities and other properly constituted authorities of charges which they are authorised to make in respect of the *works*.
	53	Payments for

(a) cancellation charges arising from a compensation event

(b) buying or leasing land or buildings within the Working Areas

(c) compensation for loss of crops or buildings

(d) royalties

(e) inspection certificates

(f) charges for access to the Working Areas

(g) facilities for visits to the Working Areas by Others

(h) consumables and equipment provided by the *Contractor* for the *Project Manager's* and *Supervisor's* offices.

	54	Payments made and received by the *Contractor* for the removal from Site and disposal or sale of materials from excavation and demolition.
Manufacture and fabrication	6	The following components of the cost of manufacture and fabrication of Plant and Materials by the *Contractor* which are

- wholly or partly designed specifically for the *works* and
- manufactured or fabricated outside the Working Areas.

	61	Amounts calculated by multiplying each of the rates for people in the Contract Data by the total time appropriate to that rate spent on manufacture and fabrication of Plant and Materials outside the Working Areas.

Design	7	The following components of the cost of design of the *works* and Equipment done outside the Working Areas.
	71	Amounts calculated by multiplying each of the rates for people in the Contract Data by the total time appropriate to that rate spent on design of the *works* and Equipment outside the Working Areas.
	72	The cost of travel to and from the Working Areas for the categories of design people listed in the Contract Data.
Insurance	8	The following are deducted from cost

- the cost of events for which the contract requires the *Contractor* to insure and

- other costs paid to the *Contractor* by insurers.

Contract Data

PART ONE – DATA PROVIDED BY THE *CLIENT*

Completion of the data in full, according to the Options chosen, is essential to create a complete contract.

1 General

The *conditions of contract* are the core clauses and the clauses for the following main Option, the Option for resolving and avoiding disputes and secondary Options of the NEC4 Engineering and Construction Contract June 2017 (with amendments October 2020)

Main Option ☐ Option for resolving and avoiding disputes ☐

Secondary Options ☐

The *works* are ☐

The *Client* is

Name ☐

Address for communications ☐

Address for electronic communications ☐

The *Project Manager* is

Name ☐

Address for communications ☐

Address for electronic communications ☐

The *Supervisor* is

Name ☐

Address for communications ☐

Address for electronic communications ☐

The Scope is in

The Site Information is in

The *boundaries of the site are*

The *language of the contract* is

The *law of the contract* is the law of

The *period for reply* is   except that

- The *period for reply* for   is

- The *period for reply* for   is

The following matters will be included in the Early Warning Register

Early warning meetings are to be held at intervals no longer than

2 The *Contractor's* main responsibilities

If the *Client* has identified work which is set to meet a stated *condition* by a *key date*

The *key dates* and *conditions* to be met are

condition to be met	key date
(1)	
(2)	
(3)	

If Option C, D, E or F is used

The *Contractor* prepares forecasts of the total Defined Cost for the whole of the *works* at intervals no longer than

3 Time

The *starting date* is

The *access dates* are

	part of the Site	date
(1)		
(2)		
(3)		

The *Contractor* submits revised programmes at intervals no longer than

If the *Client* has decided the *completion date* for the whole of the *works*

The *completion date* for the whole of the *works* is

Taking over the *works* before the Completion Date

The *Client* **is/is not** willing to take over the *works* before the Completion Date (Delete as applicable)

If no programme is identified in part two of the Contract Data

The period after the Contract Date within which the *Contractor* is to submit a first programme for acceptance is

4 Quality management

The period after the Contract Date within which the *Contractor* is to submit a quality policy statement and quality plan is

The period between Completion of the whole of the *works* and the *defects date* is

The *defect correction period* is   except that

• The *defect correction period* for   is

• The *defect correction period* for   is

5 Payment

The *currency of the contract* is the

The *assessment interval* is

The *interest rate* is   % per annum (not less than 2) above the

                    rate of the   bank

If the period in which payments are made is not three weeks and Y(UK)2 is not used

The period within which payments are made is

If Option C or D is used

The *Contractor's share percentages* and the *share ranges* are

share range			Contractor's share percentage
less than	%		%
from	% to	%	%
from	% to	%	%
greater than	%		%

If Option C, D, E or F is used

The *exchange rates* are those published in

on   (date)

6 Compensation events

The place where weather is to be recorded is

The *weather measurements* to be recorded for each calendar month are

- the cumulative rainfall (mm)
- the number of days with rainfall more than 5 mm
- the number of days with minimum air temperature less than 0 degrees Celsius
- the number of days with snow lying at   hours GMT

and these measurements:

The *weather measurements* are supplied by

The *weather data* are the records of past *weather measurements* for each calendar month which were recorded at

and which are available from

Sidebar: CORE CLAUSES · MAIN OPTION CLAUSES · SECONDARY OPTION CLAUSES · COST COMPONENTS · CONTRACT DATA

CORE CLAUSES

MAIN OPTION CLAUSES

SECONDARY OPTION CLAUSES

COST COMPONENTS

CONTRACT DATA

Where no recorded data are available

Assumed values for the ten year weather return *weather data* for each *weather measurement* for each calendar month are

If Option A or B is used

The *value engineering percentage* is 50%, unless another percentage is stated here, in which case it is _____ %

If Option B or D is used

The *method of measurement* is _____

If there are additional compensation events

These are additional compensation events

8 Liabilities and insurance

If there are additional *Client's* liabilities

These are additional *Client's* liabilities

(1) _____

(2) _____

(3) _____

The minimum amount of cover for insurance against loss of or damage to property (except the *works*, Plant and Materials and Equipment) and liability for bodily injury to or death of a person (not an employee of the *Contractor*) arising from or in connection with the *Contractor* Providing the Works for any one event is _____

The minimum amount of cover for insurance against death of or bodily injury to employees of the *Contractor* arising out of and in the course of their employment in connection with the contract for any one event is _____

If the *Client* is to provide Plant and Materials	The insurance against loss of or damage to the *works*, Plant and Materials is to include cover for Plant and Materials provided by the *Client* for an amount of

If the *Client* is to provide any of the insurances stated in the Insurance Table

The *Client* provides these insurances from the Insurance Table

(1) Insurance against

Minimum amount of cover is

The deductibles are

(2) Insurance against

Minimum amount of cover is

The deductibles are

(3) Insurance against

Minimum amount of cover is

The deductibles are

If additional insurances are to be provided

The *Client* provides these additional insurances

(1) Insurance against

Minimum amount of cover is

The deductibles are

(2) Insurance against

Minimum amount of cover is

The deductibles are

(3) Insurance against

Minimum amount of cover is

The deductibles are

The *Contractor* provides these additional insurances

(1) Insurance against

Minimum amount of cover is

The deductibles are

(2) Insurance against

Minimum amount of cover is

The deductibles are

(3) Insurance against

Minimum amount of cover is

The deductibles are

CORE CLAUSES

MAIN OPTION CLAUSES

SECONDARY OPTION CLAUSES

COST COMPONENTS

CONTRACT DATA

Resolving and avoiding disputes

	The *tribunal* is	
If the *tribunal* is arbitration	The *arbitration procedure* is	
	The place where arbitration is to be held is	

The person or organisation who will choose an arbitrator if the Parties cannot agree a choice or if the *arbitration procedure* does not state who selects an arbitrator is

If Option W1 or W2 is used

The *Senior Representatives* of the *Client* are

Name (1)	
Address for communications	
Address for electronic communications	
Name (2)	
Address for communications	
Address for electronic communications	

The *Adjudicator* is

Name	
Address for communications	
Address for electronic communications	

The *Adjudicator nominating body* is

If Option W3 is used

The number of members of the Dispute Avoidance Board is **one/three** (delete as applicable)

The *Client's* nomination for the Dispute Avoidance Board is

Name	
Address for communications	
Address for electronic communications	

The Dispute Avoidance Board visit the Site at intervals no longer than [ ] months

The *Dispute Avoidance Board nominating body* is

X1: Price adjustment for inflation (used only with Options A, B, C and D)

If Option X1 is used   The proportions used to calculate the Price Adjustment Factor are

0. [   ]   linked to the index for   [   ]

0. [   ]   [   ]

0. [   ]   [   ]

0. [   ]   [   ]

0. [   ]   [   ]

0. [   ]   [   ]

0. [   ]   non-adjustable   [   ]

1.00 [   ]

The *base date* for indices is   [   ]

These indices are   [   ]

X3: Multiple currencies (used only with Options A and B)

If Option X3 is used   The *Client* will pay for the items or activities listed below in the currencies stated

items and activities	other currency	total maximum payment in the currency
[ ]	[ ]	[ ]
[ ]	[ ]	[ ]
[ ]	[ ]	[ ]

The *exchange rates* are those published in   [   ]

on [   ]   (date)

X5: Sectional Completion

If Option X5 is used   The *completion date* for each *section* of the *works* is

section	description	*completion date*
(1)	[ ]	[ ]
(2)	[ ]	[ ]
(3)	[ ]	[ ]
(4)	[ ]	[ ]

X6: Bonus for early Completion

If Option X6 is used
without Option X5   The bonus for the whole of the *works* is   [   ] per day

CORE CLAUSES

MAIN OPTION CLAUSES

SECONDARY OPTION CLAUSES

COST COMPONENTS

CONTRACT DATA

If Option X6 is used with Option X5

The bonus for each *section* of the *works* is

section	description	amount per day
(1)		
(2)		
(3)		
(4)		

The bonus for the remainder of the *works* is

X7: Delay damages

If Option X7 is used without Option X5

Delay damages for Completion of the whole of the *works* are [   ] per day

If Option X7 is used with Option X5

Delay damages for each *section* of the *works* are

section	description	amount per day
(1)		
(2)		
(3)		
(4)		

The delay damages for the remainder of the *works* are

X8: Undertakings to the *Client* or Others

If Option X8 is used

The *undertakings to Others* are

provided to

The *Subcontractor undertaking to Others* are

works   provided to

The *Subcontractor undertaking to the Client* are

works

CORE CLAUSES

MAIN OPTION CLAUSES

SECONDARY OPTION CLAUSES

COST COMPONENTS

CONTRACT DATA

X10: Information modelling

If Option X10 is used

If no *information execution plan* is identified in part two of the Contract Data

The period after the Contract Date within which the *Contractor* is to submit a first Information Execution Plan for acceptance is

The minimum amount of insurance cover for claims made against the *Contractor* arising out of its failure to use the skill and care normally used by professionals providing information similar to the Project Information is, in respect of each claim

The period following Completion of the whole of the *works* or earlier termination for which the *Contractor* maintains insurance for claims made against it arising out of its failure to use the skill and care is

X12: Multiparty collaboration (not used with Option X20)

If Option X12 is used

The *Promoter* is

The Schedule of Partners is in

The *Promoter's objective* is

The Partnering Information is in

CORE CLAUSES

MAIN OPTION CLAUSES

SECONDARY OPTION CLAUSES

COST COMPONENTS

CONTRACT DATA

X13: Performance bond

If Option X13 is used | The amount of the performance bond is

X14: Advanced payment to the *Contractor*

If Option X14 is used | The amount of the advanced payment is

The period after the Contract Date from which the *Contractor* repays the instalments in assessments is

The instalments are
(either an amount or a percentage of the payment otherwise due)

Advanced payment bond | An advanced payment bond **is/is not** required. (Delete as applicable)

X15: The *Contractor's* design

If Option X15 is used | The *period for retention* following Completion of the whole of the *works* or earlier termination is

The minimum amount of insurance cover for claims made against the *Contractor* arising out of its failure to use the skill and care normally used by professionals designing works similar to the *works* is, in respect of each claim

The period following Completion of the whole of the *works* or earlier termination for which the *Contractor* maintains insurance for claims made against it arising out of its failure to use the skill and care is

X16: Retention (not used with Option F)

If Option X16 is used | The *retention free amount* is

The *retention percentage* is _____ %

Retention bond | The *Contractor* **may/may not** give the *Client* a retention bond. (Delete as applicable)

X17: Low performance damages

If Option X17 is used | The amounts for low performance damages are

amount		performance level
	for	
	for	
	for	
	for	

CORE CLAUSES

MAIN OPTION CLAUSES

SECONDARY OPTION CLAUSES

COST COMPONENTS

CONTRACT DATA

X18: Limitation of liability

If Option X18 is used	The *Contractor's* liability to the *Client* for indirect or consequential loss is limited to	
	For any one event, the *Contractor's* liability to the *Client* for loss of or damage to the *Client's* property is limited to	
	The *Contractor's* liability for Defects due to its design which are not listed on the Defects Certificate is limited to	
	The *Contractor's* total liability to the *Client* for all matters arising under or in connection with the contract, other than excluded matters, is limited to	

The *end of liability date* is ☐ years after the Completion of the whole of the *works*

X20: Key Performance Indicators (not used with Option X12)

If Option X20 is used	The *incentive schedule* for Key Performance Indicators is in	
	A report of performance against each Key Performance Indicator is provided at intervals of	months

X22: Early *Contractor* involvement (only used with Options C and E)

If Option X22 is used   The Budget is

item	description	amount
(1)		
(2)		
(3)		
(4)		
Total		

The *Contractor* prepares forecasts of the total Defined Cost of the work to be done in Stage One at intervals no longer than

The *Contractor* prepares forecasts of the total Project Cost at intervals no longer than

If there are additional events which could change the Budget	These are additional events which could change the Budget
	(1)
	(2)
	(3)

The *budget incentive* is ☐ % of the saving

CORE CLAUSES

MAIN OPTION CLAUSES

SECONDARY OPTION CLAUSES

COST COMPONENTS

CONTRACT DATA

CORE CLAUSES

MAIN OPTION CLAUSES

SECONDARY OPTION CLAUSES

COST COMPONENTS

CONTRACT DATA

Y(UK)1: Project Bank Account

If Option Y(UK)1 is used | The *Contractor* **is/is not** to pay any charges made and to be paid any interest paid by the *project bank* (Delete as applicable)

The *account holder* is **the *Contractor*/the Parties** (Delete as applicable)

Y(UK)2: The Housing Grants, Construction and Regeneration Act 1996

If Option Y(UK)2 is used and the final date for payment is not fourteen days after the date on which payment becomes due | The period for payment is ☐ days after the date on which payment becomes due

Y(UK)3: The Contracts (Rights of Third Parties) Act 1999

If Option Y(UK)3 is used

term	beneficiary

If Y(UK)3 is used with Y(UK)1 the following entry is added to the table for Y(UK)3

term	beneficiary
The provisions of Options Y(UK)1	Named Suppliers

Z: *Additional conditions of contract*

If Option Z is used | The *additional conditions of contract* are

PART TWO – DATA PROVIDED BY THE *CONTRACTOR*

Completion of the data in full, according to the Options chosen, is essential to create a complete contract.

1 General

The *Contractor* is

Name	
Address for communications	
Address for electronic communications	

The *fee percentage* is _____ %

The *working areas* are

The *key persons* are

Name (1)	
Job	
Responsibilities	
Qualifications	
Experience	
Name (2)	
Job	
Responsibilities	
Qualifications	
Experience	

The following matters will be included in the Early Warning Register

CORE CLAUSES

MAIN OPTION CLAUSES

SECONDARY OPTION CLAUSES

COST COMPONENTS

CONTRACT DATA

2 The *Contractor's* main responsibilities

If the *Contractor* is to provide Scope for its design | The Scope provided by the *Contractor* for its design is in | [ ]

3 Time

If a programme is to be identified in the Contract Data | The programme identified in the Contract Data is | [ ]

If the *Contractor* is to decide the *completion date* for the whole of the *works* | The *completion date* for the whole of the *works* is | [ ]

5 Payment

If Option A or C is used | The *activity schedule* is | [ ]

If Option B or D is used | The *bill of quantities* is | [ ]

If Option A, B, C or D is used | The tendered total of the Prices is | [ ]

If Option F is used | Work which the *Contractor* will do is

activity | price

[ ] | [ ]

[ ] | [ ]

[ ] | [ ]

[ ] | [ ]

Resolving and avoiding disputes

If Option W1 or W2 is used | The *Senior Representatives* of the *Contractor* are

Name (1) | [ ]

Address for communications | [ ]

Address for electronic communications | [ ]

Name (2)

Address for communications

Address for electronic communications

If Option W3 is used and the number of members of the Dispute Avoidance Board is three

The *Contractor's* nomination for the Dispute Avoidance Board is

Name

Address for communications

Address for electronic communications

X10: Information modelling

If Option X10 is used

If an *information execution plan* is to be identified in the Contract Data

The *information execution plan* identified in the Contract Data is

X22: Early *Contractor* involvement (only used with Options C and E)

If Option X22 is used

The Stage One *key persons* are

Name (1)

Job

Responsibilities

Qualifications

Experience

Name (2)

Job

Responsibilities

Qualifications

Experience

The Pricing Information is in

Y(UK)1: Project Bank Account

If Option Y(UK)1 is used

The *project bank* is

named suppliers are

CORE CLAUSES

MAIN OPTION CLAUSES

SECONDARY OPTION CLAUSES

COST COMPONENTS

CONTRACT DATA

Data for the Schedule of Cost Components (only used with Options C, D or E)

The listed items of Equipment purchased for work on the contract, with an on cost charge, are

Equipment	time-related on cost charge	per time period

The rates for special Equipment are

Equipment	rate

The rates for Defined Cost of manufacture and fabrication outside the Working Areas by the *Contractor* are

category of person	rate

The rates for Defined Cost of design outside the Working Areas are

category of person	rate

The categories of design people whose travelling expenses to and from the Working Areas are included as a cost of design of the *works* and Equipment done outside the Working Areas are

Data for the Short Schedule of Cost Components (only used with Options A or B)

The *people rates* are

category of person	unit	rate

The published list of Equipment is the edition current at the Contract Date of the list published by

The percentage for adjustment for Equipment in the published list is   % (state plus or minus)

The rates for other Equipment are

Equipment	rate

The rates for Defined Cost of manufacture and fabrication outside the Working Areas by the *Contractor* are

category of person	rate

The rates for Defined Cost of design outside the Working Areas are

category of person	rate

The categories of design people whose travelling expenses to and from the Working Areas are included in Defined Cost are

CORE CLAUSES

MAIN OPTION CLAUSES

SECONDARY OPTION CLAUSES

COST COMPONENTS

CONTRACT DATA

Index

Index by clause numbers (Option clauses indicated by their letters, main clause heads by bold numbers). Terms in *italics* are identified in Contract Data, and defined terms have Capital Initial Letters.

neccontract.com | © nec 2017